PRAISE FOR KATE
AND *THE SECR*

'Splendidly paced, passiona~~te~~
Salley Vickers, *The Times*

'Here is someone who can really write.' Peter Carey

'A magnificent novel – an unflinching exploration
of modern Australia's origins.'
New Yorker

'An outstanding study of cultures in collision . . . a chilling,
meticulous account of the sorrows and evils of colonialism.'
Guardian

'Kate Grenville has transformed an Australian myth
into a dazzling fiction of universal appeal. It is a
pleasure to be able to praise a true novelist.'
Patrick White

'I had had my fingers crossed for Kate Grenville's
The Secret River to win the Man Booker: you have to
be a master to spin a story that vast, hone it to perfection
and make it all look so effortless.'
Rebecca Pearson, *Independent on Sunday*

'*The Secret River* stands out as a work of sustained power
and imagination, of poetry and insight. No truer piece of
fiction has been written about the Australian past.'
Peter Temple, *Australian*

'This is not your standard historical novel. This
is real tenderness and sympathy.'
The Times

Searching for
THE
SECRET
RIVER

BOOKS BY THE AUTHOR

FICTION:

Bearded Ladies

Lilian's Story

Dreamhouse

Joan Makes History

Dark Places

The Idea of Perfection

The Secret River

NON-FICTION:

The Writing Book

Making Stories: How Ten Australian Novels Were Written
(with Sue Woolfe)

Writing from Start to Finish

Searching For
THE
SECRET
RIVER

KATE GRENVILLE

CANONGATE
Edinburgh · New York · Melbourne

First published in Great Britain in 2007 by
Canongate Books Ltd, 14 High Street,
Edinburgh EH1 1TE

First published in Australia in 2006 by
The Text Publishing Company

1

Portrait of Solomon Wiseman c. 1820–38, oil painting,
reproduced with permission of the Mitchell Library,
State Library of New South Wales. Artist unknown, 'Wiseman's
villa' c. 1835, watercolour, S. H. Ervin Gallery Collection, National
Trust of Australia (NSW). Purchased 1981 with the assistance of the
Garden Committee. Reproduced with permission.
Map by Tony Fankhauser

British Library Cataloguing-in-Publication Data
A catalogue record for this book is available on
request from the British Library

ISBN 978 1 84767 002 1

Design by Chong
Typeset in 11.5/16.3pt Janson by
J&M Typesetting
Printed and bound in Great Britain by
Clays Ltd, St Ives plc

www.canongate.net

For Nance Isobel Russell,

1912–2002,

who gave me this journey

Contents

PART ONE

I
Wiseman's Ferry

In the puritan Australia of my childhood, you could only get a drink on a Sunday if you were a 'bona fide traveller'. That meant you had to have travelled fifty miles or more. Around Sydney a ring of townships at exactly the fifty-mile mark filled with cheerful people every Sunday. One of them was a little place called Wiseman's Ferry.

It was called that because its cluster of houses and shops stood on the south bank of the Hawkesbury River, at a point too wide to be easily spanned by a bridge. For the last two hundred years, anyone wanting to cross had taken a ferry. The original ferryman was a man named Solomon Wiseman.

He was my great-great-great grandfather.

It was Mum's idea to go and look at the place, one autumn

day when I was about ten—it would have been around 1960—not because it was Sunday and she wanted a drink, but because of her feeling about family history. She'd heard a few stories about Solomon Wiseman from her mother, who'd got them from her mother, and so on back for five generations. Some families hand down christening mugs or silver teapots. We inherited stories.

She was proud of them: not of the stories themselves so much as the fact of having them. She enjoyed knowing the exact ways she was connected to the past along the family tree, and being able to tell a few anecdotes about some of those forebears.

All four generations had been rough country people—right up to her parents, who'd run a succession of pubs in country towns. There were several convicts in the family tree. She was proud of them. They'd shown a bit of spirit, she thought, in trying to get something for themselves and their families. They were survivors.

Remarkably for her time and background—both her parents had left school at fourteen—Mum had scrambled into an education. She'd trained as a pharmacist and married our father, then a young solicitor with political leanings.

Now we lived in a big old house with a glimpse of Sydney Harbour. The roof leaked, the bathroom was a lean-to out the back, and the house was earmarked for demolition by the Department of Main Roads, but it was built on a generous scale. Mum had a dressmaker who made her copies of stylish—even outlandish—clothes from pictures in French magazines (the green brocade evening-coat made in panels so it hung like a piece of sculpture, the organza cocktail dress with the over-sized collar that stood up around the back of her head). But her thrifty country childhood was never far away. She kept every piece of string and rag, she darned the elbows of her jumpers and she scraped the last speck off the butter-paper, using it later to line the cake-tin. She was a vigorous, intelligent, original, plain-speaking woman with a clear sense of what mattered and what didn't.

One of the things that mattered was keeping those family stories alive.

Solomon Wiseman had worked on the Thames, but ran foul of the law in some way and was transported to Australia. Once in Sydney, he quickly won his freedom and, the story went, took up land on the Hawkesbury River. He'd done well for himself and died a rich man.

The best bit of the story, as far as I was concerned, was the part about his wife Jane. Wiseman was supposed to have killed her by throwing her down the stairs of the house he'd built on the Hawkesbury. Her ghost was rumoured to haunt it.

So, when Mum suggested a day at Wiseman's Ferry to see the land Solomon had settled on and the house he'd built, I was keen. I pictured something Gothic and spooky. Creaking doors. Faded bloodstains. Maybe even the ghost herself.

I was short-sighted, but nobody knew. I was a teenager before anyone—myself included—realised that I badly needed glasses. Anything further away than a metre was a blur. As a result, my memory of the day at Wiseman's Ferry is a series of close-ups and details. Nothing hangs together.

I remember a long dull drive through fuzzy bush, Mum exclaiming at a view that I couldn't see (I thought that being able to appreciate views was something that happened when you got old, like enjoying oysters and olives). An alarming series of hairpin bends zigzagged down the side of a valley, the river swimming greasily at the bottom. The little township—a dozen houses, a shop or two, and the pub—was terribly quiet, steaming under a sultry sun, and with that humming silence you get in the country.

The house that Wiseman had built was now the pub, a sprawling two-storey stone place, with verandahs all around, top and bottom. From the bar I could hear a murmur of male voices and the races on the radio. Being so young, I wasn't supposed to be in a pub, so it felt as if we were breaking the rules when Mum took me by the hand and led me inside.

There were the stairs. They must be the ones down which Jane Wiseman had fallen. Mum pointed and marvelled, and I peered. To my short-sighted eyes the flight of steep and narrow steps seemed to stretch up forever into darkness. It was easy to imagine the argument, the angry shove, and the woman tumbling down step after step, head over heels, skirts tangling.

Mum made a *tsk tsk* noise and shook her head, the way she did when she disapproved. 'You can see how it happened, can't you,' she whispered. 'Poor thing wouldn't have had a chance.'

I'd never been clear whether the story implied that Wiseman killed her accidentally or on purpose. Mum's *tsk tsk* could have meant either. I remember squinting up at the stairs and choosing not to ask.

I didn't ask, partly because I'd heard the story so often that I should have known. If I asked now, it would be obvious that I hadn't ever been paying attention. And partly I didn't want to know. The idea of a dramatic death in the family was all right, the idea of a ghost even better. But I wasn't sure I wanted a murderer for a great-great-great grandfather.

Plus I wanted to get outside. The bar was right beside us. Any moment the publican would come out and there'd be a scene. He'd go, 'Now what do you think you're doing,' and Mum would say, 'Look we're not doing any harm,' and I'd stand there trying to be invisible.

Outside, Mum showed me the stone lions on the tall gateposts. 'He brought them specially from England, they cost him a hundred guineas.'

The lions were invisible to me, but I nodded. I may not have been able to make the lions out, but I was close enough to the stone gateposts to see the way each block was pecked and pocked with grooves.

'That's where they worked it with the picks,' Mum said. 'The convicts he had, assigned servants.'

That was real to me: that close-up detail. Each block of stone had a hundred pick-marks, two hundred, five hundred. I could picture it: a man standing in the steamy sun, swinging the pick again and again to square off the lump of sandstone. And, when he'd got it right, he'd have to start straight away on the next one.

I remember running my fingers into the grooves, wondering how anyone could have put up with it.

Later we went off in search of the graveyard. The story included something about Wiseman having been buried with a box of sovereigns at his feet. That sounded interesting, but finding the graveyard was a matter of driving along dusty yellow roads through dusty grey bush. Every time Mum saw a person, she'd pull over. 'We're looking for Solomon Wiseman's grave,' she'd say. 'He was my great-great grandfather.'

I'd see their faces open out in surprise, they'd stare extra hard at her, they'd peer into the car to have a look at me, and point away up another road.

What was it I could detect in their faces as they examined us a bit more closely than they needed to?

Cows wandered along the verges of those roads, and Mum stopped every time we drove past a cow-pat that didn't look too wet. She'd get out and pick it up and put it in the sugar-bag that was always in the back of the car. I slid further down in the seat. 'Don't be silly, lovey,' she said. 'It's not dirty, only grass, wonderful for the garden.'

At last we found the graveyard. In my memory it's a blur of trees and grey headstones until I got up close. Then I could see where the stonemason had ruled guide-lines in the stone: exactly like the lines I drew myself, when I had to do a heading in my Social Studies exercise book, except that I rubbed them out when I'd done the words. But these chiselled lines were still sharp. The letters themselves were a mixture of 'little' and 'big', the way I'd written when I was in Infants. Some of the words were spelled oddly: did 'Henery' mean 'Henry'? Now and then the stonemason had left out a letter by mistake and had to put it in above the word, with an upside-down v to show where it should go.

'They probably couldn't read or write,' Mum said. 'Copying it off a bit of paper. You'd get it wrong, you wouldn't know.'

From that day at Wiseman's Ferry, that's all I remember. The steepness of the stairs, the labour of the picks, and the misspelled names of the dead. The past: another country. Nothing to do with me. A day that was too hot and steamy, the smell of cow manure ripening in the car.

It was forty years before I went back.

2

Walking for Reconciliation

May in Sydney is a cold windy month, and the morning of 28 May 2000 was colder and windier than usual. On that day, the Sydney Harbour Bridge was closed to traffic and, along with 200,000 other people in beanies and scarves, I walked across it to show that I supported the idea of reconciliation between black and white Australians.

I'd have been hard pressed to say exactly what I thought reconciliation meant. It had something to do with what had gone on in Australia over the last 200 years: the violence, the taking-away of Aboriginal children from their parents, the fact that we descendants of Europeans lived on land that had once belonged to other people. Beyond that it was all uncertain: should we feel guilty, should we be talking compensation, what about treaties and land rights?

The Bridge straddles Sydney Harbour, its northern foot a short walk from the house where I'd grown up, its southern foot beside Sydney Cove where the city itself had begun. In 1788, Captain Arthur Phillip, in charge of a fleet of ships full of convicts, had dropped anchor in that cove, run the Union Jack up a flagpole, and declared Britain the owner of the whole lot.

The Bridge had come to stand for Australia, the icon that identified us around the world. Traditionally much of what mattered in Australia had come from Britain. We were proud of the fact that the engineer in charge of building the Bridge— a great technical feat—was an Australian. We knew the history of its opening day in 1932. The premier was lifting the scissors to cut the ribbon when a man called de Groot, who disapproved of the premier's politics, galloped up and slashed the ribbon with his sword. It was a swashbuckling story that gave the Bridge a personality.

So the idea of having the Reconciliation Walk across the Bridge—with all its affectionate associations—was a potent one. The walk itself promised to be another big symbolic thing. Its aims were large and vague enough to make us feel cosy in spite of the bitter westerly wind. Everyone was smiling. We were all pretty pleased with ourselves.

We—myself and a friend and our children—strolled along the roadway with the crowd. I was thinking more about Mum than about reconciliation. She'd often told me her own story about the Bridge. She was a young pharmacist when it was to be opened, and had been given the afternoon off—a rare treat—to join the crowd walking across it. She claimed to have seen de Groot ride up on his horse with his sword held aloft.

She'd always said, though, that she might just have seen the picture in the paper the next day.

Almost at the end of the walk, on the southern end of the Bridge, I noticed a group of Aboriginal people leaning against the railings watching us. A couple of men with hats and spreading beards, two or three women with their skirts pressed against their legs in the wind. At the end of the row, a tall handsome woman frankly staring, as if to memorise each face. Our eyes met and we shared one of those moments of intensity—a pulse of connectedness. We smiled, held each other's gaze, I think perhaps we gestured with our hands, the beginning of a wave.

It should have made me feel even better about what I was doing, but it sent a sudden blade of cold into my warm inner glow.

This woman's ancestors had been in Australia for a long time. Sixty thousand years was the current figure. Her ancestors might have been living on the shores of Sydney Harbour when the First Fleet sailed in.

The blade I was feeling was the knowledge that my ancestor had been here too. Solomon Wiseman hadn't arrived on that first convoy, but he'd arrived within twenty years of it. His ship would have anchored in this bay. He'd have come ashore right underneath where an Aboriginal woman and I were exchanging smiles.

And what if *my* great-great-great grandfather had glanced up, and seen *her* great-great-great grandfather standing on a rock watching the new arrivals? I didn't know much about what had gone on between the Aboriginal people and the settlers in those early days. And yet I was sure that Solomon Wiseman wouldn't have smiled and waved at any Aboriginal man watching him come ashore.

I hadn't thought for years about that out-of-focus visit in my childhood to Wiseman's Ferry. Now, for the first time, I wondered what had happened when Wiseman had arrived there and started the business of 'settling'. Until this moment it had never occurred to me to wonder who might have been living on that land, and how he'd persuaded them to leave it.

In that instant of putting my own ancestor together with this woman's ancestor, everything swivelled: the country, the place, my sense of myself in it.

The wind had got stronger and colder as we'd walked. It was ruffling the harbour the wrong way, making the water a hard dull metal. I wanted to get away from it all now: the smiles, the benign feeling of doing the right thing, the shuffling crowd of people whose pleasure in the moment hadn't been sliced open.

I urgently needed to find out about that great-great-great grandfather of mine. I needed to know what he was like, and what he might have done when he crossed paths with Aboriginal people.

Until I knew that, it felt like nothing but wilful blindness—even hypocrisy—to go through the symbolic motions. The imagery of our walk, across a bridge, suddenly seemed all too easy. We were strolling towards reconciliation—what I had to do was cross the hard way, through the deep water of our history.

This is the story of what happened when I took the plunge and went looking for my own sliver of that history.

When the Reconciliation Walk took place, I'd just published my fifth novel, *The Idea of Perfection*. I hadn't yet started another.

This was unusual for me. In the past, the end of one book had always overlapped with the beginning of another. I had a horror of a gap, as if fearing that if I stopped writing I might never start again.

But this time there was no new novel on the horizon. I wondered if I'd written all that I had in me to write.

When I decided to look for Solomon Wiseman and his dealings with the Aboriginal people, I thought there might be a non-fiction book of some kind in the material—perhaps something like a biography of Wiseman and a portrait of his times. I didn't know what, if anything, I'd find, or whether there would be enough of interest for a book. This would be something I would do just for myself, because I needed to know.

Whenever Mum had told me the family stories about Solomon Wiseman and his descendants, I'd hardly listened, could never get the generations straight in my head, forgot the details.

But something of her passion to keep those stories alive must have conveyed itself to me, because a few years before the Bridge walk I'd sat down with her and recorded the stories into my cassette player.

When our two children were babies, Mum minded them a couple of days a week so that their father, Bruce, and I could work. They loved going to her place because she truly believed in children *playing*, in them finding their own play. One day either Tom or Alice got hold of a roll of toilet paper and when I came to pick them up it was everywhere, looped around the backs of the chairs, winding in and out of the stair-rails, out the window and back again. Mrs Next-Door had visited, apparently, and was scandalised.

'But,' Mum told me, 'I said to her, what toy could you ever buy that would keep a child so interested?'

I'd arrive at her house in the morning, and she'd have made me sandwiches and a thermos, as she did when I was at school. I'd drive off, park in a quiet spot overlooking the harbour, and get into the back seat with one of the children's kickboards across my lap by way of desk. It was a fine way to work: the children happy with their Granny, the thermos and sandwiches a comfort, and that stunning view. I did some good work there.

The children were unpredictable sleepers, and when I got back they'd sometimes be napping in the pram that Mum called The Magic Box. Mum and I would have a cup of tea while we took it in turns to wiggle the pram and keep the baby asleep. Now and then I'd get out the little cassette recorder and ask her to tell me the family stories again.

She was unafraid of the machine, unself-conscious about being taped. She spoke easily, telling those well-worn stories one more time. I got her to tell me about Solomon Wiseman, and then about the generations between him and us. For each generation there were a few vivid stories: the newly arrived Cockney boy who had to drive three rams from one end of Goonoo Goonoo Station to the other—'without a dog!' Granny Davis, who always had a gun loaded in the corner of the hut on account of the blacks: 'not to use it, just to show them she had it'. Auntie Rose, who had shared one pair of boots with her four sisters 'so they could never all go into town at the same time'.

About her own life she was less comfortable. There were regrets, mistakes, loneliness; deaths and divorces. Her voice lost its confidence, the words grew dull. I had to prompt her with questions, but she didn't always want to answer. 'I don't really remember,' she'd say, and we'd move on.

I'd never played those tapes back, but a few days after the walk I got them out and began to listen. Mum was older and frailer now: the tapes reminded me how strong she'd once been. In the background a child would grizzle from time to time and I could be heard going *shhh, shhhhh*. It was good to hear Mum laugh as she told the story about herself as a girl, putting castor oil on her eyelashes to make them grow.

You could hear in her voice the pleasure she took in telling the Wiseman story once more, knowing that this time it was being recorded. Hearing it again, I realised that, although I thought I'd forgotten every detail, at some level I knew it by heart:

Solomon Wiseman was born in London and worked on the docks. He married, and for some offence we don't know of, he was transported to Sydney, arriving in 1806 on the *Alexander*. I've heard that he was a smuggler, but I don't know for sure. His wife accompanied him, which suggests money. He was not only freed but given a grant of land at what is now called Wiseman's Ferry. He started the ferry, made money, built the hotel that's still there—the two lions at the gate were brought especially for the house from England. His first wife died and he married a local girl and had a number of children, one of whom was called Sarah Catherine, my great-grandmother. Strong rumour was that he killed this first wife by throwing her down some stairs. Her ghost is supposed to haunt the place.

Solomon Wiseman was said to be an extremely cruel man. He had a number of assigned convicts to work for him. It is said he had a big rock on his property, which was called Judgment Rock and he used to sit there in judgment on offenders. Even in a harsh and cruel age perhaps he was cruel—the fact remains he was hated and feared. Not that that prevented a rather flowery obituary from being published.

Sol had a number of children by his second wife and by this time he would have been well off, sufficiently so to give his daughters a riding master. My Auntie Rose—and I think my mother too—told the story of one of these girls being seduced by the riding master, becoming pregnant and being thrown out of the house. They thought both she and the baby died and you could hardly marvel at it—what would a girl do in those terrible days?

This story had been passed down the family from Granny Davis, through Granny Maunder and Auntie Rose and at last to my mother. Mum always used exactly the same phrases each time she told it. The story was like a little sealed capsule that couldn't be jarred open with questions.

I was glad it was there, though. It was like Grandma's sideboard that had sat out in the hall in our house throughout my childhood. Its drawers smelt of mothballs, the top was marked with a blue stain in the shape of Tasmania, its wooden handles were cracked. But when I looked at it I saw a penumbra of associations, memories, stories. That was what made it precious. Mum's version of Solomon was solid like that sideboard, even though its details could seem foggy and unreal. It gave me a sense that my ship was anchored to the past by ropes of story.

3
The Mitchell Library

The Mitchell Library stands just up the hill from where the convicts were put ashore. It was built in an age when Ancient Greece was the pinnacle of civilisation and Ionic columns announced Culture. Its main Reading Room is a vast lighted box, radiance pouring down from the ceiling.

A week after the walk across the Bridge I climbed its steps and pushed through its big bronze doors. The Mitchell contains most of the documents relating to early settlement in New South Wales. If there were any information about Solomon Wiseman that might start to fill the void that had opened up in me, that's where I'd find it.

From trips to the library as a student years before, I knew it housed a Family History Centre. I'd glanced in and seen how busy it was. Most of the people there seemed to be middle-aged women, their eyes shining, the thrill of the chase upon them as they went looking for ancestors.

I didn't go in. I'd always thought they were a bit of a joke, those ladies in their cardigans tracking down every twig of their family tree. Now that I was one of them, I wanted even less to go there.

My mother's story was full of gaps. That 'offence we don't know of', for example—I assumed that finding out more would involve expert delving into arcane catalogues and long-forgotten documents. So, instead of the Family History Centre, I went to the area within the Mitchell Reading Room where original material was accessed, a silent place behind its own set of glass doors, sealed off from the main part of the library.

The librarian heard me out politely, then pointed to some shelves behind me lined with small white boxes of microfilm. 'See over there? Old Bailey Session Papers. The transcripts. Just start at 1806 and work backwards.'

There they were, on the open shelves. You didn't even have to fill out a Request Slip.

I realised that, like Lord Nelson, the family story had been holding the telescope up to its blind eye. It pretended it didn't know why Solomon Wiseman was sent to Australia. But it made sure that it contained the two details that made it easy to find out: the date of his arrival and the name of the ship he came on.

If it was so easy to discover, why had no one tried before?

The first thing on the microfilm for 1804–06 was an index of the trials, arranged by date, everything in solid old type. The 'WHOLE PROCEEDINGS' were 'Taken down in shorthand by Blanchard and Blanchard'.

I skimmed the list. I wasn't really expecting to find Solomon. Something about these tidy boxes, these alphabetical lists, sat awkwardly with the family story. It was as if Grandma's sideboard, blue stain and all, was put on display in a museum.

There was something else, too. I wasn't sure that I *wanted* to find him. My hand on the creaking handle of the microfilm reader, the soft sounds of the library around me, I realised that my comfortable ignorance was about to be undone. If I found Wiseman's trial, I could never tell my children that 'for some offence that we don't know of, he was transported to Sydney'.

And what else might there be for me to know? What about that other question, the one about the Aboriginal people? I'd bowled in to the library lightly enough. But my quest was a bit like wanting the doctor to be entirely frank. You only wanted her to be entirely frank if she had good news.

The trouble with knowing was that it wouldn't end there. What did you do with what you knew? You could hide it away again, but you'd know you'd done that. You couldn't ever go back to not-knowing.

I was starting to see that, if I went on with this, I'd come up not only with Solomon Wiseman's place in the scheme of things, but my own. When you were a white Australian, investigating your own history could lead you into some murky territory.

No wonder my hand was turning more and more slowly.

When 'Wiseman, Solomon' leaped off the page at me, I felt a pulse of fright. Relief, too, as I read: 'Crime: Stealing on board a Ship or Barge on the navigable River Thames'.

Wiseman's was quite a long trial. It was complicated in its details, but the outline was simple enough. He was thirty years old, a 'lighterman' on the Thames, in the employ of one Matthias Prime Lucas. On April 10, 1804, Wiseman took Lucas's lighter—some kind of small boat, I assumed—down to a ship at Horseleydown and loaded it with valuable 'Brazil wood'. He was supposed to take it up-river to Three Cranes Wharf and unload it there.

Around midnight my great-great-great grandfather rowed to Three Cranes Wharf with the wood. It was a very dark night and he didn't know that Lucas, along with some other men, was following him in another boat. Lucas had obviously been tipped off.

At Three Cranes Wharf, Wiseman tied the lighter up and climbed onto the wharf. Lucas heard him call out 'Ned!' and say, 'Damn your eyes, Ned, why did not you come down to lend a hand with the lighter?', and someone answered that he 'could not come any sooner, he come as soon as he could'.

Wiseman and Ned started to unload the Brazil wood—but instead of putting it up on the wharf, they were moving it into another boat.

Lucas and his friends heard it all: 'The next sound I heard was, apparently to me, as though a log of wood was scraping over the gunnel of the lighter, as if a person was easing it down, we then heard a hollow sound as if it was set down on the floor at the bottom of the barge.'

They waited until a few pieces of wood had been moved, then they rushed out of their hiding-place. Lucas described what happened next: 'I struck at Wiseman with a small hanger; he retreated back from me, and said, pray do not, for God's sake, or words to that effect; I did not attempt to pursue the blow, but thought of closing with him, and taking him by the collar; I sprang towards him, the oars of the barge were then lying sloping from the fore-beam, and…I did not observe the oars; I fell over the oars, and he jumped into a little boat.'

But Lucas had laid his plans well, and had an employee, Richard Rowey, waiting in a small boat nearby. Rowey recalled: 'I heard Mr Lucas's voice calling out, Rowey; after which I discovered a boat coming from where the lighter lay… I followed them, and when they came to Crawshay's wharf…I got on board of theirs; one man jumped overboard; I told him I would shoot him, if he attempted to make his escape. Not hearing any more of him, I supposed he was drowned.'

I laughed aloud at this matter-of-fact tone. In the hushed air of the library it seemed a loud noise, rupturing the calm of books and papers with rude life. At his desk the librarian lifted his head and looked at me, and the woman at the next table gave a little cough.

Rowey was still talking. 'I turned my attention to the prisoner at the bar; he exclaimed, for God's sake, Mr Rowey, have mercy, you know the consequence, or something to that effect; he then stepped on the aft athwart of the boat, and made a spring into the river; he got hold of my boat, which I had left, and made his escape.'

Like everyone else, Wiseman got his moment to speak in his own defence. 'After I brought that lighter up, I left her, I did not see her afterwards; I meant to come to her at high water; I left her when…I heard there was such a piece of work about her, I was afraid to come back; Mr Lucas knows no lighter upon the river could come to her.'

My great-great-great grandfather's voice, speaking directly across nearly two centuries! The actual phrases he used! And all those others: Lucas with his pompous rehearsed account, Rowey rattling off something as if learned off by heart, Ned whining his excuses. They leaped off the page, these people— their words, their tone! They crowded around me, their voices singing out clearly into my ear, indignant or strident or pleading.

It was as if I'd opened the bronze doors under the classical pediment and released a crowd of people into the demure Mitchell Library: shouting and sweating, galloping along the floors, insisting on having their say.

The prisoner called seven witnesses who gave him a good character, but the verdict was Guilty and the sentence was Death.

When I'd finished reading Solomon's trial, I sat for a long time in front of the machine. The yellow light poured down onto the screen, an island of light in the darkened microfilm corner. I felt as if I'd just seen a snake or narrowly avoided being run over: in shock.

He was so alive, a person frightened of death, flustered by the court so that his Prisoner's Defence came out in a muddle. I could hear him breathe, feel the heat of his body as he stood in the dock of the Old Bailey.

In an hour I'd learned more about him than Mum had ever known. I'd burst out of the sealed capsule of the story she'd so carefully transmitted. I was on my own now: on my own, with this man I hardly knew.

I had a huge hunger to know more. What sort of life did he have in London? Why did he steal when he knew the *consequence*? Was he desperate, or greedy?

I decided to spend some time on the internet. The Mormons—for whom genealogy is important—have a massive database of births, deaths and marriages. It's all online: you type in a name and a date and, bingo, there's your ancestor.

The name was easy. The date wasn't quite so certain: at the trial his age was given as thirty, but I thought this might have been approximate, so I searched a few years either side.

It was a shock to find twenty-nine Solomon Wisemans. I decided to ignore the ones not born in London (although my Solomon Wiseman might not have been born there) and weeded out the repetitions. Even when I'd done that, there were still seven.

I printed out the search results and began to study them.

Several Soloman Wisemans were born—in different years—in Bermondsey. Several had parents called William and Elizabeth, one had parents called William and Catherine. One had parents called Richard and Jane. Two were born—in different years—in Bermondsey and had a spouse called Jane. One was born in Essex and had a spouse called Jane. One was christened at St Mary Mounthaw, wherever that was, another at St Mary Somerset. One record asserted that Solomon Wiseman had married Jane Middleton at Spitalfields Christ Church in 1799. Another gave him an address—Butler's Buildings, Bermondsey—and a son baptised at St Mary Magdalene, Southwark.

I already had two Solomon Wisemans: my mother's and my own. From this search I now had nine. But somewhere behind my sources—the family story, the Old Bailey records, and these terse and perhaps unreliable entries on the Family Search site—was the real man. He had lived and died not as a story or a set of entries on a website, but an individual as precisely himself as anyone I knew. I hungered to find out who he was.

The search for him pointed towards London and, by a stroke of extraordinary luck, at just that time I had the opportunity to go there.

4
Centenary of Federation

At the beginning of the twentieth century, the separate colonies that made up Australia federated into one nation. It was a big moment in our brief history.

The Australian government marked the occasion of the Centenary of Federation in many ways. There were re-enactments: of the arrival of the First Fleet, of the opening of the first Parliament. All over Australia, country towns strung up bunting and had parades in period costume. And in London there was to be a showcase of Australian culture in June 2000. There'd be wine and dance, paintings and theatre. And writers, a dozen of us, giving readings and talks on the South Bank.

One of the writers was a young Aboriginal woman I'd met once before, Melissa Lucashenko.

We first met at a literary festival—the writer David Foster introduced us. Since then I'd read some of her fiction and essays. She is a terrific writer and a thought-provoking essayist.

Like many white Australians, I'd never really known any Aboriginal people. I'd met the poet Oodgeroo Noonuccal, and the actor and dancer David Gulpilil. In my long-ago days as a film editor I'd worked on a couple of documentary films on Aboriginal subjects and I'd met the people involved. But I'd never had a sit-down conversation with an Aboriginal person. (Not knowingly, anyway: I'd probably met plenty of Aboriginal people without being aware of their ancestry.)

So when we arrived in London for the Centenary of Federation, and I spotted Melissa having lunch in a café near the hotel, I asked if I could join her.

Rather to my surprise, she remembered our meeting, and made space beside her at the table. We hadn't been talking long before she asked, 'Where's your family from?'

I stared at her, could feel my mouth open trying to find an answer. She watched me and waited.

At the next table a man crouched over his plate of pie and chips as if afraid someone might snatch it away. Along from him two women pursed their lips towards their thick cups of tea at the same moment, like synchronised swimmers.

In my mind Melissa's question was unfolding into other questions. What family do you mean, me and my brothers and parents? Or family in the sense of grandfathers and great-grandfathers? What do you mean *from*? From Sydney, where I live now? From Gunnedah, in northern New South Wales, where my mother was born? From London, where my great-great-great grandfather was born?

I had no answer, and turned the question back to her. It turned out not to be simple for her, either. Her father's family was Ukrainian, her mother's family were Bundjalung people. She lived in Brisbane, but her country—Bundjalung country—was the far north coast of New South Wales. That was where she was from.

I was surprised by a sudden savage envy. In spite of all the damage that had been done to indigenous families and their connection to their country, she could go to a particular spot on the planet and say, *this is where I'm from*. So could all those English people around us: that man feeding chips into his mouth as if it were a shredder, the synchronised sippers, now both sliding the cups onto their saucers. If you asked them, they'd probably be able to tell you about some village in Cheshire or Yorkshire or Wales where their ancestors were buried. That would be where they were from.

So I sat gawping at Melissa, who was waiting for me to work out a response to the simplest question in the world. By way of answer, I told her a bit of the Wiseman story. 'My great-great-great grandfather was born in London...' I began. I got to the bit about 'he was freed and took up land on the Hawkesbury'.

'What do you mean "took up"?' she said. 'He took.'

He took up land on the Hawkesbury. They were the words from the family story: a formula, unquestionable. I'd been repeating them for years.

Took up: you took up something that was lying around. You took up something that was on offer. You took up hobbies and sports.

Took had many more possibilities. You took something because it was there, like a coin on the ground. You took offence or flight or a bath. Or you took something away from someone else.

The words *took up* were standing in for some set of actions. The words weren't the thing itself, they only pointed towards it. The thing itself lay behind the words, an object behind a screen. Of course I'd always known that. But the lack of fit between a word and the thing it stood for had never before come to me like a punch in the stomach.

Took up—suddenly it felt like a trick.

The trick itself was bad enough. The fact that I'd let myself be taken in by it was worse. Melissa and I had exchanged such small and harmless words. *Family. From. Took up.* But they were turning out to be grenades.

Twenty-five years earlier, I'd arrived in London on a working holiday visa. For my generation, it was what you did: you went to Britain, because Britain was what you knew. I'd grown up learning by heart the Kings and Queens of England, the Principal Industries of Nottingham and Sheffield. I knew all about daffodils and cuckoos, about Biggles and the Battle of Britain. The cultural landscape of my generation was almost wholly British. It made for an awkward lack of fit between the cultural landscape—so vividly real in your head—and the one outside the window.

So it was a relief, twenty-five years ago, to be in the place where they matched. I saw daffodils fluttering and dancing in the breeze, I heard my first cuckoo of spring, I felt the dread as a sunless English winter closed in.

It felt that I'd come home.

I bought English clothes and an ancient English bicycle,

heard myself acquiring something of an English accent. Would rather have died than go to see the changing of the Guard, the way mere tourists did. Would rather walk for miles, getting more and more lost, than stand on a street corner with a map in my hand. My day was made if someone mistook me for a local and asked me the way.

I eked out my visa with all kinds of casual jobs: I wrote captions for the illustrations in textbooks, edited documentary films, worked as a typist for companies that made soft drinks, computer printers, sheet music. I wasn't looking forward to the day my visa would run out and I'd have to go back to Australia.

Eventually, though, I came home. I'd changed, but so had Australia. Migration from all around the world had transformed an outpost of Britain into something more complex. The national anthem no longer began 'God save our gracious Queen' but 'Australians all, let us rejoice'. We were writing books, making music and doing paintings that were something other than imitations of what was happening in Britain. No one seemed to have heard of Biggles any more.

I was glad to be part of this new thing that was happening. I got on with work and family and made a good life. I couldn't imagine living anywhere else.

So being back in London after a quarter of a century was an odd and complicated feeling. I met my earlier self around every corner—that person who'd felt like a stranger in her own country, who wouldn't acknowledge that she was really a foreigner here, in England.

I'd told Melissa about this feeling and said that I was planning to do some research into family history while I was here. After our conversation, it felt even more important to find out more about that shadowy man, Solomon Wiseman.

5

The Society of Genealogists

I imagined that this family history business would be tidy: a matter of stepping from one fact to another. I had an idea of myself as an orderly researcher, with index cards and colour-coded folders. The past could be put together like a jigsaw puzzle, I thought: take enough time, have enough patience, collect enough facts, and it would all make a picture.

The logical place to start was at the beginning. Where was Wiseman born, and when?

Like so many London addresses, the Society of Genealogists was a kind of intelligence test. When next day I finally found the street called Charterhouse Buildings—a cul-de-sac full of rubbish bins somewhere up beyond St Paul's—I felt pretty cocky. I *was* an old London hand, after all.

It was a tall thin building and, being so tall and thin, inside it seemed to be mostly narrow, lino-covered stairs that strained and popped as people went up and down, pressing themselves into the corner of the landing to let each other pass. The Births, Deaths and Marriages Room on the second floor was busy. Behind the counter, elderly gentlemen in tweed—volunteer genealogists, I discovered—were helping the customers.

Someone had unfolded a long scroll of sticky-taped paper with an endless family tree tracking down page after page and was poring over it with one of the tweedy gentlemen. A woman like me, with too many coats and bags over her arm, kept saying, 'No, it's the distaff line I want, d'you see? The distaff line.' A tremulous old man was trying to use the equally ancient photocopier in the corner. A volunteer was explaining, 'It costs 20p, but you put 10p in and give me 10p, cos it doesn't take 20p.' The old man turned over the coins in his palm, first one way, then the other.

When it was my turn, I thought it would be plain sailing. I had brought my seven Solomon Wisemans with me to London. The most likely seemed to be the one born in 1776 and baptised at St Mary Mounthaw. My plan was to ask for the registers of the church.

But my gentleman—a scholarly fellow with leather elbow-patches—frowned as if at news of a death. 'St Mary Who?'

I repeated the name.

'Never heard of it,' he announced, and that was going to be that, but I was able to bring forth from my shabby bag the printout from the Mormon website.

He frowned over it for some time, even turning it over to see the back, which wasn't much help as I'd been recycling my paper and the back announced *Ms Ford's Year Six Farewell*

Please Bring A Plate. Finally he consulted another, sterner man.

In front of me across the counter they compared abstruse names. 'Have you looked in so-and-so?' 'Yes, and I tried the Register of such-and-such too.' At last in a small shabby book, they found it.

No one had ever heard of St Mary Mounthaw because the church was destroyed in the Great Fire of London. Its parish was later joined with St Mary Somerset—another name from the Mormon records. Where were the parish records for St Mary Somerset? More consulting obscure books, more riffling through indices and cross-references.

St Mary Somerset, it turned out, was also destroyed in the Great Fire. It was rebuilt by Wren soon after, but was demolished in 1872 and the parish united with St Nicholas Cole Abbey.

I seemed to be getting a long way from Solomon Wiseman.

St Nicholas Cole Abbey was gutted by a firebomb in May 1941. *Uh oh*, I thought, *there go the parish registers*.

The search was no longer mine, however. There were now no fewer than four gentlemen activated by my enquiry. Between them all, they performed some little bit of genealogical legerdemain and directed me to the proceedings of the Harleian Society, Volume 58, Shelf MX/R58.

I sat down at one of the big brown lino-covered tables, along with the other searchers burdened with raincoats and bags, and took a deep breath.

Volume 58 of the Proceedings of the Harleian Society consisted of lists of baptisms, births and deaths for St Mary Mounthaw. Feeling on the edge of some momentous discovery, I turned the pages.

Suddenly there he was, in the christenings for 1776: May 26, Solomon, s. of Richard and Jane Wiseman, Rector James Jones.

I stared at the words, straining after feeling. None came. This wasn't Solomon Wiseman. These were marks on a page, nothing more. I copied them into my notebook, just the same, and stared, wanting them to split open and reveal the person behind the name: a red-faced baby, crying at the cold touch of water from the baptismal font, the mother ready to spring forward in case James Jones dropped her son, the father shifting from foot to foot, impatient to get back to his afternoon with…no, I was making it all up.

I flipped backwards and forwards, looking for other Wisemans, and found plenty.

1772, May 15, Mary, daughter of Richard and Jane Wiseman.

1767, April 26, Elizabeth, daughter of Richard and Jane Wiseman.

Were these the sisters of Solomon? Elizabeth, eleven years old, suddenly popped into the picture around the font, wearing…what *did* they wear? Beside her, Mary, aged four, held the edge of her sister's dress with one hand and picked her nose with the other. Did the sisters make a pet of the new baby, carrying him on their hips, arguing about whose turn it was to push him in the pram? Did they have prams? Or were they the other kind of big sister, the secretive hair-pulling and ear-pinching kind?

Outside the window, the low grey sky had decided to let out some rain. The building site next door speckled and darkened and I could see people on the street two floors below pointlessly turning up their coat collars. I was in no hurry to go out into the rain, so I opened more of the proceedings of the Harleian Society.

I tried the baptismal registers of St Mary Somerset, which swallowed up the parish of St Mary Mounthaw. It had a whole string of Wisemans.

1749, February 4, Robert, son of Solomon Wiseman by Dorothy.

1751, December 8, Sarah, daughter of Solomon Wiseman by Dorothy.

1753, December 23, Solomon, son of Solomon Wiseman by Dorothy.

1756, March 7, John, son of Solomon Wiseman by Dorothy.

1758, January 4, Anthony and Elizabeth, twins, son & daughter of Solomon Wiseman by Dorothy.

1760, Catherine, daughter of Solomon Wiseman and Dorothy.

1762, September 5, Robert, son of Solomon Wiseman by Dorothy.

1774, May 15, Dorothy, daughter of Richard & Jane Wiseman.

1783, April 6, Robert, son of Richard & Jane Wiseman.

1788, June 6, Elizabeth, daughter of Robert & Elizabeth Wiseman.

1789, November 8, Sarah, daughter of Robert & Elizabeth Wiseman.

1791, February 6, Elizabeth, daughter of Robert & Elizabeth Wiseman.

Thinking how hard poor Dorothy Wiseman worked at producing a child every two years for so long, I looked at the burials. Elizabeth, Sarah and Anthony all died within a short time of Dorothy having children of those names.

Then I noticed something else. Unlike the baptisms, the burials were arranged alphabetically. In looking for Wiseman I noticed other, similar names such as Wistham and Wiseham. A Solomon Wistman of Long Lane, Bermondsey, was buried on April 9, 1769. This was a year after the birth of a Solomon Wiseman in 1768. Was it possible that this was the same person?

With horror I realised that Solomon Wisemans were starting to proliferate like weeds in every parish, recorded under any variant of his name that semi-literate clerks might dream up. My Solomon Wiseman might be any of them, or none.

I replaced the blue artificial leather books on their shelves, put my coat on and thanked the tweed volunteers. As I left, one of them gave me a pamphlet: *Searching for your Convict Ancestor*. I stuffed it into my bag.

It was still raining. Out on the street, where the buses were roaring up and down Clerkenwell Road, I seemed to hear Solomon Wiseman laughing.

Later I sat on the bed in my hotel room and assembled everything. I ignored all the quasi-Wisemans—those Wistmans and Wisehams—hovering around the object of my search. With the new data (or perhaps-data) from the Society of Genealogists, I was going to arrange all the Wisemans into some kind of coherence.

It was infuriating. The same names and dates and places recurred with small variations. I had the maddening feeling that all these interlocking pieces of information could join up—but I didn't know how. There had to be a pattern, because Solomon Wiseman really had existed.

It took a while, but I came up with a scenario. I counted six Wiseman households in London. Four of them lived north of the river, in the parish of St Mary Somerset. Of these four couples, three had sons named Solomon. So, by 1790, there were four Solomon Wisemans living in a small area a stone's throw north of the Thames: a man of sixty-seven; his thirty-seven-year-old son; a fourteen-year-old; and a newborn.

Meanwhile, south of the river, more were multiplying. There were two Wiseman couples within a mile of each other. These couples produced three Solomons between them. In 1790, as well as those four Solomon Wisemans north of the river, there were two more in the south: a boy of thirteen and a newborn. Another Solomon Wiseman, from the same address as the thirteen-year-old, was born in 1768 but died a year later.

To get even to this degree of coherence, I had to kill off wives and make their husbands re-marry. I sent families backwards and forwards across the river. Fathers and uncles gave their own names to sons and nephews, infants died and their names were given to the next child born. I cursed the eighteenth century's niggardly way with the same few names: Sarah, Catherine, Richard.

I drew up my scenario on a fresh piece of paper and propped it up at the end of the bed. I made a cup of hotel tea and sat there sipping and admiring. It had been enjoyable, like solving a crossword puzzle.

By the time I'd finished my tea, the exhilaration had faded. My intricate scenario made sense of the information, but that was all. The information might not be correct, and it was almost certainly not complete.

Let's face it, I told myself. All I can be sure of now is exactly what I knew before: Solomon Wiseman was born, in some house or other, of some mother and father or other, in some year or other. All I've done is tell a story.

I realised, though, that I'd learned one very useful thing: not about Solomon Wiseman, but about searching for the past. I'd learned the difficulty of establishing even the simplest fact. *Solomon Wiseman was born in London*…that had always seemed so solid. Now it felt like the opening line of a fairytale.

My education had taught me to look for a bedrock of verifiable data on which to build. This process was teaching me to be more humble. So far I'd found nothing that was absolutely certain. The transcript of the trial was a fact. But it recorded only what was said in court—who knew what really *happened* on that dark night in 1804, or why?

Constructing a story to accommodate all those Solomon Wisemans, I'd learned something else, too: how strong the urge was to make sense of things. The desire to find a pattern could overwhelm the reality that there might not be one.

Now, sitting on my bed in the hotel room, I remembered the pamphlet from the Society of Genealogists. 'Finding out more about the convict,' I read. 'If you really want good quality personal information about a convict, then you would be better advised to look for an application for clemency.'

Solomon Wiseman had been sentenced to death, but was reprieved. Perhaps he had applied for clemency.

'Applications for clemency often included just the kind of details about personal circumstances and family background that family historians want to know. They can be found in the collections of the Public Record Office at Kew.'

Family historian? I still rejected that idea of myself, but I wasn't too proud to go to Kew.

6
The Public Record Office

I took the train the following day. Kew was a quiet and tidy suburb of small semi-detached villas. Pairs of squat milk bottles on every front step. Shiny brass letterslits in the front doors. Neatly clipped hedges and gauze curtains, with grand pianos and blond children visible beyond them. And a great suburban silence hanging over everything.

Suddenly the streets fell away, a void opened up and the Public Record Office sat in front of me like a mother ship come to earth. In the blankness of its gaze, the bareness of its surrounds—square ponds with toy-like ducks gliding on them—it resembled nothing so much as a prison.

Or was it that prisons and hangings were on my mind?

The Public Record Office, like the Society of Genealogists,

was one long intelligence test.

Within the echoing polished limestone of the vast entrance hall, dwarfed by space, I stood at a counter that was just a bit too high—I was actually on tiptoes—and filled out a form. Down on the other side was a man whose eyes never met mine and whose pale face showed no expression during our whole interaction.

In exchange for my form I eventually got a small laminated card and moved on to the next part of the test. A sign told me that in the Reading Room I could use only pencils, so, feeling rather clever, I bought some from the woman at the shop. Another sign told me that I couldn't take my bag in. Fair enough, and there were the lockers. The lockers needed a coin and I didn't have the right change, so I went back to buy another pencil. The woman was waiting for me, pencil in one hand, locker-coin in the other.

Upstairs, kindly women with glasses dangling on large bosoms explained how to register myself on the computer and order my documents. First, though, I had to find my documents. Guided by the women I looked up big green folders of 'class lists'. This meant documents of different classes: the class I was after was called 'Home Office, Series 17-19, 48, 54 and 56: Petitions'. I entered my request through the computer. Then I went next door into a sort of glass room within a larger room, and joined another queue to get my Reader's Number.

It was a long queue and it wasn't moving quickly, and after my experience at the entrance desk, and with the women with the dangling glasses, I wasn't confident I was in the right place.

'Is this where I get a Reader's Number?' I asked the man in front of me.

'Indeed it is,' he said. With the slowness of the queue we got chatting. He had white hair, a red face, a vaguely sailorish kind of beard. 'It used to be just dusty scholars here,' he said. 'Now everyone's interested in medals and family history or they're Australians and New Zealanders looking up their ancestors.' He gave me a look: a twinkle-in-the-eye sort of look, an I've-got-you-worked-out sort of look.

I was irritated at this smug sailor-man, annoyed that he'd stereotyped me as that comic cliche, the middle-aged Australian lady looking up her ancestors, probably in search of a duke.

HO 17/423 consisted of a brown cardboard box tied up like a Christmas present with pink tape and embossed with a crest and 'Supplied for the Public Service': old-fashioned, austere. Someone out of Dickens might have had a box like this.

Inside was a leather-bound volume, a little bigger than foolscap size, not a book so much as a folder, with original documents, all different shapes and sizes and weights of paper bound into it. This wasn't exactly 'leather-bound'. That was a familiar concept of tooled volumes with the titles in gilt and marbling on the endpapers. At the fund-raising fete for the children's school, someone occasionally donated a leather-bound book to the secondhand bookstall. It was always snapped up early by one of the dealers.

This was not like that. This was something a good deal more earthy. You could still see the pores of whatever animal it was, the places where hair had grown. This was not so much leather as *skin*.

Inside, the first sheet of paper said, 'There is no doubt that this is the first register of Criminal Petitions in the Home Office.' Then a signature and the date: 1894.

I liked that tone. As I turned the page I had a fleeting picture: there they were in 1894, a whole lot of dusty clerks in some high-ceilinged room in the Home Office, slanting sunlight coming in from high windows, the rods of light floating with dust. The head clerk had a box on the table in front of him—no, a tin trunk. He'd blown an inch of old dust off the lid and prised it open. Inside was a jumble of documents, higgledy-piggledy, some torn, some speckled with damp, some in bundles tied with pink tape.

'Now then,' he said, or words to that effect. 'We're going to sort this lot out. You, Wiggins, put them in date order. The first hundred will be the first volume. Here, this will be the first page.' Drawing a piece of paper towards him and dipping his long nib into the inkwell, he wrote, 'There is no doubt that this is the first register of Criminal Petitions in the Home Office.' As all the clerks watched, their long pale unhealthy faces expressionless, he signed it and added the date: 1894.

As I turned through the pages I realised that these were petitions all right, but not for clemency. I wanted to stop and read them, but I had to get on.

Yet another box. Who last undid this string? Inside, a big book with a hard white cover like plastic, scored and deeply scratched as if bricks had been grated across the surface. Perhaps this book went through the Blitz. Even the folder of historical documents had a history.

These were petitions for clemency. I could feel my heart thudding.

I turned through the documents scanning the impossible

old spidery writing for dates and names. Some were in beautiful clerk's copperplate, every word a minor calligraphic masterpiece. In some, the salient words were written in red ink, with summaries in the margin, the whole finished with a blob of sealing wax. Others were in unreadable scrawls like a doctor's prescription: you could spend a week deciphering it. These came as a shock, they seemed so modern. On some, the ink was still black and emphatic; others had faded to the palest brown. Some were written on flimsy paper, sometimes only a half-sheet with a few lines scrawled in the middle. Others were on thicker material: could this be parchment, one of those words I'd spent my life reading without ever coming across the object? A few were written on some stiff and glassy-surfaced substance that I guessed might have been vellum.

All were bound together in whatever way they fitted, right way up or sideways, and folded where necessary to fit within the cover. They were in very approximate date order.

As a system of appeal, it looked pretty haphazard. The appeal for one John Allen, for example, seemed to rely on the fact that 'he is a fine tall handsome young man'. But the key to success seemed to be who you knew, not who you were.

By late afternoon I was tired and my eyes were aching and dry. I hadn't found any petitions on behalf of Solomon Wiseman. I had a nasty flat feeling of having wasted a whole day and given myself a headache for nothing.

The place didn't close for another hour, though, and I'd never be back here again. I opened the book at random, flipped through a few. I found one the right way up and in an easy hand. An intensity of horror came flaming off the page at me:

My deare and loveing wife I write this hart brakeing letter
to inform you the shameful and scandalous distress I have
brought upon you and my poore unhappy children wich I
am afraid in a few Days will be Fatherless and you a poor
Unhappey Distressed Widdow by the unhappey death I am
likely to bring upon myself; had I takin youre advice on the
Sunday night not to go with Groombridge to Crawley
Faire this shame would not have happened but now I must
bare the Eshew of it be what it will the judge cast five for
Deth out of Eight as went to Lewes from Horsham Gaol
but repreived three before he left the town and left
Groombridge and myself for execution and not to look for
any mercy I should wish you to see Gen Watson witch I
think by Petition I may git a Pardon and be comfortable
with Family once more and as to my confinement &
distress of mind will bring me to my Right Understanding
so in the sum of looking upon it as Troubles I shall account
it as given from the God above as a scourge for my past
offences and after you have seen Gen Wattson and advised
with him I make no doubt but he will give you a Coppy of
a Petition I trust Gen Wattson to be my ondly friend to do
his utmost as he knows more of distress than any man
liveing I trust to him to be my friend in the name of the
Lord I am to die I should wish to see you once to take my
unhappy farewelle of you and my deare children if you can
git Halls horse and Cart git Roles to come down with you
and Jane the coach here is 6 or 7 shillings down so I think
hors and Cart will be cheapest when you come down go to
the Sine of the Crown W Howes and he will come to the
gaol with you and can sleep that Night at Mr Howes If we
are to be executed it will be on next Saturday fortnight My

best wishes to G Wattson and his Family and all who ask after me From your unhappy distressed but loveing Husband
  Wm Boon

  This is wrote with allmost a broken hart so don't mind the badness of Writeing But now I think of it you not see W. Ives til after the Assizes Go to see the Gen first but see W. Ives for he may be a friend this being my first offince.
  Send me a answer by the return of post
  Horsham Gaol
  Sussex

As I copied out William Boon's letter with one of my many pencils, it seemed I was re-living his anguish. The poor man's thoughts were all over the place, from God to the price of a horse and cart in the same moment. I could hear the sweaty terror of what was happening, the panic to end this bad dream, the desperate effort to think clearly.

Boon's letter was followed in the book by one from General Watson, appealing on Boon's behalf to Lord Hawkesbury. Then some minion of Lord Hawkesbury forwarded the general's letter to the original trial judge, who replied: 'I have perused the petition of William Boon, and the other papers left therewith: and I am humbly of opinion that he is in no wise the proper object of the Royal Mercy.'

A wave of grief overwhelmed me there at the quiet desk in the Public Record Office. William Boon's letter had lain there for two hundred years. He was dead, his wife and children were dead, General Watson was dead. And yet William Boon himself was more real to me than many of the people I knew. His howl of regret echoed down the years.

What could you do for so much distress in the past? It

seemed wrong to turn away from it, close the book, kill it all over again. The only thing I could do was copy it out: tell the story. It didn't change anything, but it felt like an act of respect.

All the way back to the hotel on the Tube it was as if William Boon was beside me, a living, speaking man. My search for facts about Wiseman had been fruitless. They were there, somewhere, and if I knew more about how to look, I might even have found them. But my meeting with William Boon was telling me I didn't have to approach the past in a forensic frame of mind. I could *experience* the past—as if it were happening here and now.

Staring out from the train at the Thames, gleaming darkly under a lowering yellow sunset, I decided to suspend the paper search for Wiseman. Instead I'd look for him in the places where the past had happened: the lanes and streets, the churches, and above all the river.

7
Three Cranes Wharf

I nearly didn't bother to try to find Three Cranes Wharf on a map. To expect to stumble on a place mentioned in the Old Bailey transcript of so long ago seemed ridiculous, like finding a Neanderthal cave, bison-paintings and all, in the basement of a skyscraper.

But two centuries in London was nothing more than a slow blink, and you didn't need an antique map of London to find Three Cranes Wharf. It was right there—as Three Cranes Walk—on page 94 of my *London A to Z*, alongside Southwark Bridge.

The next afternoon the Centenary of Federation was able to manage without one of its writers: I had a couple of hours to myself. Guidebook in one hand, umbrella in the other, I made my way towards Three Cranes Walk.

Down there in the East End, by the river, was where some of the worst of the bombing took place during World War II. Now it was all big blocky office buildings in undistinguished 50s and 60s architecture. Street names, like archaeological remains, were the only evidence of what had once been here: Bread Street, Milk Street, Pudding Lane.

Until the last hundred years you'd probably have been able to see the river from all these streets, glinting between the low tight-packed buildings and the grey stone churches. All that remained now was the fall of the land, the streets flowing down the hill like streams.

I followed the slope but at the last moment, just when I thought I'd get to the river, I was blocked by a multi-lane road buried between office buildings. The din of trucks, motor-bikes, cars at speed, was unremitting. I was conscious of how frail my body was compared to the lorries, the blank-eyed cars and the deafening bikes hurtling along this tube of bitumen.

No one ever waited for the traffic lights to let them cross as long as I did at Lower Thames Street, E3. By the time I got to the other side I felt shellshocked.

There still seemed no way to reach the river. A solid wall of buildings lined the road. If not for the map, fluttering in my hand in the slipstream from the lorries, I wouldn't have guessed the river was there, a building's thickness away.

With some sense of finding a sanctuary, I turned towards a church. It was like so many others: grey limestone, streaked and smeared with poisoned rain, some columns holding up a portico.

Down a narrow alley beside the church, a man in a stained polo shirt, an airline bag across his chest, was crouching to pick up a scattered mass of cigarette butts. He dropped them into his bag and scurried on, head down, scanning the footpath and the gutter.

Apart from the polo shirt and the plastic airline bag, he might have stepped out of Wiseman's London. Wiseman himself might have walked here, stood under this portico to shelter from the rain. I laid the palm of my hand on the rough limestone, feeling the cold grit on my skin. His hand might have lain there too, leaving molecules behind, wedged in the grain of the stone, as he leaned on it talking to someone, or waiting for someone, or...what? Smoked a pipe? Drank from a flask in his pocket? Scratched the nits in his hair?

Bolted to one of the columns was a splintered piece of wood so old it was black and stone-like. A corroded plaque told me it was a piece of the 'original Roman bridge over the Thames that once stood close to this site'. I stepped back and looked at it with more respect. Roman. Julius Caesar might have cast an eye over this same piece of wood. He might have leaned on it when it was part of the bridge, talking to someone, or waiting for someone, or scratching the nits in his hair.

This thing was two thousand years old. In Australia, it would be behind glass in a controlled atmosphere. Machines with flickering needles would be monitoring the humidity. Strings of children would be trailed past it. They'd be invited to marvel at the fact that those adze marks had been made by someone whose mother tongue was Latin.

Here, it was bolted roughly to the side of the porch, held up with steel brackets, out there on the street with the traffic roaring past a few steps away.

Was there so much history in Britain that it could be

treated casually? There weren't enough glass cases to hold it all. Was it a more transparent history, too, with none of the uneasiness that I was feeling about Solomon Wiseman?

I looked around and saw one of those ornate black-and-white church clocks high up on the wall. I stared at it, and was just working out that it said a quarter to five, when a voice spoke right into my ear from behind: quiet, pitched to slide underneath the hysterical traffic.

'Nice old clock, isn't it?'

I hated him even before I turned and saw him. He was shortish, with receding crinkly sandy hair and one eye higher than the other, a Punch-and-Judy sort of face, features somehow too prominent, his eyes too wide open.

He was obviously a crazy. What other sort of man would come up and speak into your ear like that?

The street was suddenly empty of another human soul. The river of traffic wouldn't be stopped by someone running out and calling for help. I was frightened.

I reminded myself that I didn't have to be mild-mannered Kate Grenville, respectable wife and mother, courteous to all. I could be anyone I pleased here on Lower Thames Street.

Abrupt, right into his face, I said, 'Do you know where Three Cranes Wharf is?'

He was startled. Took a step back. 'More or less,' he said after a moment. He was watching me curiously now, as if I were the strange one.

'Well, where is it?' It was exhilarating being this rude.

'Too complicated to explain,' he said. 'But it's down there.'

I didn't believe him. He wanted to lure me into that shadowed alley. I started to move away.

'No,' he called. 'Down here.'

I hesitated and we stood staring at each other.

He was wearing one of those speckled rubbish-coloured jackets, with a checked shirt and the kind of tie that doesn't go with anything. His trousers bagged at the knees. He carried a worn and empty-looking briefcase of the old-fashioned kind with a flap over the top. His forefinger was curled around it as if to keep it from springing open, even though this briefcase would never spring open but only sag from its handle.

I wrote a whole story about him as I glanced at that sad finger. 'Here, son,' the father said as he gave him the shiny new briefcase, too embarrassed to kiss or embrace or even shake hands, only giving a hard slap on the boy's puny shoulders. 'Now you've started at work.' The father dying, of course, but the son hanging onto the relic, having it stitched crudely at the shoe-repair place when it started to go on the corners, the memory of his father embedded in the worn old thing.

Now he was a seedy balding middle-aged man trying to pick up a frowning tourist in Lower Thames Street, and wondering what he'd got himself into. 'Why do you want to find it?' he asked.

'Just a bit of family history,' I said, a fraction shamefaced now, half-regretting my rudeness. 'A family connection.' I didn't want to launch into the whole story about Wiseman in case I couldn't get rid of him.

'Look, it's down here,' he said again, and turned away without waiting to see if I was following. At a rapid speed he led me into what seemed like the inside of one of the faceless office blocks, into a kind of tunnel underneath. We turned a corner and the traffic noise was cut off. I could hear our two sets of footsteps fast on the pavement. He led and I followed a few yards behind.

This was stupid. If I disappeared off the face of the earth here, there'd be no one to guess where I'd gone.

But I kept following, at a distance. He led me across a laneway, down some stairs, along an alley between two towering office blocks, round a dogleg. Through another tunnel with a blast of chlorine. A delivery van idling and a black man with a white bag of laundry. A sudden smart glass doorway: 'Lotus Club'. Under an archway into a courtyard I glanced up and saw a naked stone woman holding a bunch of grapes in each armpit. We went beneath a long brick arch and suddenly we were out on a walkway, a building above and behind us, the river below, and a big black-and-white sign on the railing: 'Three Cranes Walk'.

The man glanced at me, then turned and was off without looking back again, left right left right with his briefcase slapping against his leg.

'Thanks,' I called, but it was too late.

Three Cranes Walk was at the foot of a massive office building. Behind me, pressing down, was the blank bulk of the building. You could imagine someone insisting, *there must be public access*. Oh, okay, they'd have said, and added this narrow thoroughfare to the plans. Beyond the railing, a wall dropped away sheer to a black muddy beach affair. Beyond that the river ran sulkily under the low grey sky.

There was a bad feeling here, as if you were right on the edge of a cliff. I hung onto the metal railing, feeling it cold under my hands. The air was full of the constant roar and hum of air conditioners, the thrum of a building working at full blast.

Somewhere close by something was beeping and clanking. A steel container was rumbling down a gantry with a spooky smooth movement. The jaws of the machine released the container onto a tarry barge, then with a whirr slid back up again. No human was anywhere in sight, only this big dangerous piece of machinery with a life of its own. But somewhere in that featureless building people were controlling it: the inheritors of Wiseman's trade, getting stuff into and out of boats as they had done for hundreds of years.

It was here, I told myself, trying to whip up a frisson. *He was right here, sweating with fear. Right here.*

I went back to where the walkway crossed the last courtyard, looking for a way to get down to the river, and saw a tall iron gate, conveniently ajar and, on the other side of it, steps going down to the shore.

Stepping through the gate took me into another place altogether. In front of me was a shore of dark grit, stones, glistening slime, then the turbid water of the river. A sudden fresh wind blew against my face. The air-conditioning noises, the traffic noises, dropped away.

The wind funnelling along the river reminded me that, underneath the streets and sewers and polite squares of grass, an earlier place was buried. London was once a wild estuary, gulls crying overhead, wading birds thrusting their long beaks into the mud, and the wind, the constant wind flattening the beds of reeds, the stunted marshy shrubs on the shore. A great pewter sky would have hung like a bowl over the eternal flatness of it, the grey water meeting the grey sky, and at low tide the sheen of cold mud would have framed the metallic water.

The current scoured downstream: fast, hard, dangerous, coursing away towards the sea. Under this lowering sky, the Thames was not benign or pretty. It was a brown and murky river, visibly ferocious. Its teeth tore around the bridge piers, bulging and splitting into white against the stone. Big iron buoys moored in the middle of the stream bobbed against their chains as the water surged around them. The Thames was no toy. The Thames could kill you without even trying.

Boats churned up and down: dragonfly-quick launches, low-slung barges throbbing away against the current making the buoys dance in their wake. There were cruisers, half-cabin boats, Water Police, Metropolitan something-or-other, and now and then a speedy powerboat bouncing along the rough water. Tourist boats with unintelligible syllables of commentary coming at me in snatches on the breeze, people stiff with chill staring at the river, at the woman standing at Three Cranes Walk trying to think about her great-great-great grandfather.

A duck nipped past me, bobbing along on the tide, swivelling its head to look at me, its round eye unblinking.

Beside the steps was a pile of stuff washed up against the wall—rounded brown pebbles, shiny black ones, dark twisted lumps of what looked like coarse glass with bits of sand and stone melted into it. Glass from the Blitz? Another layer of history, all those images of London burning?

There were shards of terracotta, smoothed by the river, all the same thickness, many with a hole in them about the size of a pencil. Old roof tiles, I thought. The hole was for tying the tile onto the battens. Maybe very old. From Wiseman's time? From Wiseman's house?

I picked one up. A bulge along one side recorded where someone had flattened it against a straight edge. The inside of the hole was grooved where a rough stick had been pushed through the clay. Feeling guilty, I slipped one into my pocket. There could be some special ordinance that forbade the pocketing of historical shards from the banks of the navigable River Thames.

I made my way between the muddy rocks and grit to the water's edge. Down there I could see what I hadn't from the steps—that the water was running along the side of a thick beam, the edge of some ancient dock that over the years had rotted away to this line of black wood, inches above the water.

As if someone had nudged me, I suddenly realised, *he was here. This, right here, where I'm standing, is where it happened.*

I stared at the wood: hard, shiny with slime. How old was it? How long did it take timber in the Thames to turn to stone? If it was as old as it looked, it could have been where Wiseman's foot rested as he called up, 'Damn your eyes, Ned, why did you not give me a hand with the lighter?' But perhaps wood decayed quickly on the tide-line of the polluted Thames. Perhaps this was only a hundred years old. Or fifty.

Maybe I should save my awe.

But what did it really matter if Wiseman's feet stepped on this exact piece of wood? Anything in the world has been trodden on by someone or other now dead and gone. The dust blowing around London must still contain molecules of Dickens' whiskers.

The tide was extremely low. This slimy wood, those broken bits of roof tile—all of it would usually be under the water. At almost any tide but this, there would have been nothing to see but brown water lapping against the top of these steps. By chance I was there at the one moment when the curtain of water was drawn back.

Later, the writers I was travelling with had a drink together and I got out the bit of roof tile to show them. It went from hand to hand, everyone's thumb smoothing the surface, everyone trying to fit their finger into the hole. 'Is this all?' someone asked. 'You didn't find anything else?'

Melissa looked at it for a long time, turning it over and over as if she were searching for something. She handed it back to me. 'So where will you go next?'

8
Lightermen

Not far from Three Cranes Wharf was the Watermen's Hall, home of the Company of Watermen and Lightermen of the River Thames. It was on St-Mary-at-Hill, a short steep street near Billingsgate fish market.

The building was narrow, two storeys high, with a lot of nicely carved stone and a majestic double door. Most of the first floor was taken up by a leadlight window with a coat of arms that looked like two angry fish beside a rowing boat, in a sea of frills from which a brawny arm emerged.

Inside, it was clear that a person enquiring about an eighteenth-century ancestor had come at a bad time. The Watermen's Hall was hired out for grand corporate functions, and one of these was happening that night. In an office cluttered with filing cabinets and desks overflowing with papers, a harassed young man was trying to answer six phones while also dealing with the builders. No, he couldn't let me see the back rooms. No, he had no information about the history of the Company.

Behind him, I could see a room with glass cases and, like the most innocent seeker after knowledge, I asked if I could have a quick look around while he got on with the phones.

He assessed me for a long moment. Hair: a mess. Shoes: tourist walkers. Clothes: dowdy respectable. Disposition: obsessive. Another phone rang. 'Oh all right,' he said. 'Just for five minutes.'

Inside were two glass cases, one containing a gigantic model of a windjammer made of carved bone, the other with a model of a rowing boat. Several enormous oars hung on hooks on the walls. There were some dim woollen jackets with a lot of elaborate piping and braid.

I glanced quickly at these dull things and heard all the phones ring imperiously, including a mobile playing 'Men of Harlech'. I thought it was probably safe to explore a bit further.

Beyond the room with the glass cases was a hallway. This had a seriously old look—worn flagstones, tongue-and-groove planks on the walls, a chill pre-damp-course sort of feeling. A narrow pew ran down one side as if to accommodate a line of people waiting.

The hall led to a curving staircase, as graceful as a twist of orange peel, its handrail gleaming, not with polish but with a couple of hundred years of hands sliding up and down it. To the surprise of a couple of burly builders doing things with buckets full of rubble, I whipped out my camera and took a few snaps.

I didn't want to push the harried young man beyond his patience, so I retreated to the room with the glass cases and was staring at the bone windjammer when he came in. He ushered me back to the office, and would have shooed me right out the door except that the phones started up again.

While he was answering them, I noticed a locked glass case full of things you could buy—watermen's ties and buttons, mugs with the coat of arms. I could see a book there: *The Life and Character of Thomas Mann, Honest Waterman of St Katherine-by-the-Tower*. I wasn't especially interested in an honest waterman, only a particular dishonest one, but I decided to buy it. It gave me an excuse to go on waiting for something to turn up.

He was such a nice young man. He was pleased I was going to buy the book, partly because it soon became obvious that no one had ever wanted even to look at anything in the case, much less buy anything out of it, and partly because if I bought something I might then leave.

The only snag was the key.

He looked in all the drawers of all the desks. He looked in the filing cabinets and the cupboards. He looked on various hooks and shelves. Finally he turned to me, apologetically. No key. End of the road.

I knew he could try harder and, if it weren't for the builders and the phones, he would. I mentioned that I was keen to buy it because my ancestor, a convict sent to Australia, had been a lighterman…Now I had his attention. All the way from Australia! In that case, we *must* find the key.

He looked again, more thoroughly, in all the drawers. He opened the safe and fossicked in there. He rang up someone else to ask. It appeared that the only human being on the planet who knew where to find the key of the locked glass case in the front office of the Watermen's Hall was Old Harold. Old Harold was on an errand somewhere, and would be back at some unspecified time.

I nearly didn't wait. The book was looking less fascinating every moment. I wasn't interested in a tie or a mug. But something kept me standing there, trying to stay out of the way of the builders as they massed in the tiny room wanting to know what to do about the junction box.

The minute Old Harold arrived, I knew it was worth the wait. Old Harold was a man not very much older than myself. He was a smiling balding person of great calmness of presence. I got the feeling that Harold had been waiting all his life for someone to come along who found the watermen as interesting as he did. That person had now appeared, in the shape of a dishevelled woman from Australia.

Old Harold found the key, I bought the book and waited till the young man was busy on his mobile. Then I quietly asked Harold whether I could have a look around. Harold—with a quick glance at the young man—jerked his head sideways. I followed him through the room with the glass cases, out into the stone-flagged passage, and up the lovely staircase.

At the top of the stairs he stood back to usher me into a big peaceful room. A radiant window filled one wall, the watermen's crest glowing on it. Under it, three enormous wooden tables were arranged like a judge's bench. Whiskery gentlemen frowned out of gravy in gilt frames on the walls.

Harold told me that this was the room where, as a

would-be apprentice to the Company of Watermen and Lightermen, he'd been 'bound over' some forty years earlier. The masters, daunting men in black suits, sat up behind the table quizzing the boys about the river rules.

'They had the fire going,' he said. 'And we had to stand here, hard up against the fireplace. It was that blessed hot, the seat of me pants was just about on fire.'

But Harold got through, and Solomon Wiseman must have, too.

Would Wiseman have been bound here, or in some earlier version of the Watermen's Hall? According to Harold, it would have been in this same room. Wiseman would have come up that staircase. His hand would have added its share to the patina of age on the handrail.

Harold was a warm, clever and generous man, bemused that I was taking notes about the day his trousers nearly caught fire. Harold's father and his father's father had been watermen. His family had lived in Bermondsey as long as anyone could remember. He was proud of his skills and knowledge, of the hard work he'd done, of getting through those tough apprentice years. Harold knew who he was, where he'd come from, and what part of the world he could claim as his own.

It was from Harold that I learned how to find out exactly when and where Solomon Wiseman was born. Since he had served an apprenticeship, his binding—including his date of birth—would be in the registers up the road at the Guildhall.

The Guildhall Library turned out to contain every kind of document, picture, map and book relating to the City of London and its guilds.

It didn't take long to find him: bound 17/12/1795, place of

birth Southwark Christ Church, April 27, 1777, master Thomas Evans Gash, freed 06/01/1803.

And in the margin, a single word in a coarse script: DEAD.

One glance had taught me more than all that time on the internet and at the Society of Genealogists. Of the many Solomon Wisemans who'd flirted with me behind the gauze of dates, churches, and parents' names, not one was my great-great-great grandfather. I could take the piece of paper which I'd so proudly propped up on the bed at the hotel, make it into a small ball, and throw it away.

Now that I knew about the Guildhall Library, I'd mine it for all it could tell me.

From the many dense volumes of Henry Humpherus' *History of the Origin and Progress of the Company of Watermen and Lightermen of the River Thames*, first published in 1869, I learned the difference between 'watermen' (they transported people) and 'lightermen' (they transported goods). I learned how Old London Bridge (still standing in Wiseman's day) choked the river so much that at low tide it created a fall of water like rapids. I read Boswell's account of choosing to get out of the boat and walk around, rather than dangerously 'shoot the Bridge'. I learned that the watermen were famous for thievery and 'foul oaths'. Unfortunately Mr Humpherus was too delicate to write down the exact words that constituted a 'foul oath'.

In the Guildhall's collection of pictures was an engraving of a waterman standing up to his knees in the river steadying his boat and watching his customers board. The gentleman— a puny slip of a fellow with dark curls—was saying to his lady, 'Be cautious my Love, don't expose your leg!' but her white-shod leg, with its dainty green high-heeled slipper, seemed displayed for the boatman's pleasure, and from the look on his face he was getting a good eyeful.

There were smudgy old maps with names you'd never dare to invent: Pickle Herring Stairs, Gun & Shot Wharf, Horselydown Old Stairs, Tattle Alley.

A few twentieth-century lightermen left memoirs in which they recalled their apprenticeship binding:

> I was still getting my 'river hands'. One very old gentle-man (one of the master lightermen) who, from the look of him, had passed the century mark years ago, managed to mumble, 'Blisters healed, sonny?' I shook my head and held out my hands, which were puffed-up from all the heavy rowing. There was a general laugh at this, they all thought it blasted funny, except me.

And gave instructions on 'tapping a cask':

> The majority of men carried 'screws' (gimlets) and as cargoes were often wine, rum and gin, the drink was cheap. Tapping a cask could be done without showing any evidence from the outside. 'Do it clean' was the maxim, by gently tapping the hoops toward the tapering end, then boring two small holes. After the 'waxer' had been drawn, the holes were neatly splined, and the hoops hammered back over the holes and secured.

These stories were from the 1930s, but something told me that nothing had changed all that much for the Company of Watermen and Lightermen since Solomon Wiseman's day.

I'd always assumed, from the family story, that being a lighter-man was an unskilled job, something you learned on the run, the only qualification being a strong back: like being a builder's labourer in my own world. When Wiseman was described in the trial as a 'journeyman lighterman' I'd taken this to mean a kind of day-labourer, journeying from one job to the next.

It made it easier to be sympathetic. In a world with no social security, no free education, no hope for a poor man, there was Wiseman, rowing his heart out on the Thames, scrounging such work as he could, living on the sweat of his brow until his health gave out—my heart always swelled with indignation at the thought of him so doomed by the accident of birth. He was no angel, but a 'journeyman lighterman' without the killer instinct wouldn't have lasted a week.

Now I was learning that a 'journeyman' is by definition someone who has served an apprenticeship. That made it the equivalent of being a plumber or an electrician rather than a builder's labourer. Not right at the top of the social ladder, perhaps, but not at the bottom by any means, and with the economic leverage of someone working in the closed shop of the guild system.

And yet—if being a journeyman lighterman was the equivalent of being a plumber today, would he have risked death to steal that Brazil wood?

The image of Wiseman was doubling, trebling, quadrupling: the Wiseman who was desperate, for whom the risk of death was worth taking; or someone else, with a skill to sell, a long way from starvation.

Wiseman came and went among the pages of the books, and I was starting to feel more and more earnest and ridiculous, trying to pin him down. Disoriented, too, like standing in the surf and feeling a swell lift you up, weightless, drifting where the sea will take you.

9
The London Poor

My time in London was nearly over, and I was filled with panic at the idea of leaving without learning everything I could. Each new piece of information led to another, and the more I was finding out, the more I wanted to know.

The day after the visit to the Guildhall Library I asked the hotel for a wake-up call. By seven o'clock I was on the Tube with the other early risers, on my way to Aldgate East and Christ Church Spitalfields. According to the Mormon website, Wiseman had married there in 1799. He was twenty-one. His bride was Jane Middleton, age unknown, described as 'a spinster of the parish of Stepney Spitalfields Christ Church London'. That entry might not be accurate, but in the absence of other information—and the time to find it—

I was going to act as though it was.

Christ Church Spitalfields was on page 87 of my now dog-eared *London A to Z*. Whitechapel Road, familiar from the Monopoly board of my childhood, was around the corner. The church was made of white limestone, the blurred creamy stone piled up in blocks and arches and columns, a child's building-block tower. Inside, gloomy grandeur; columns going up and up and vanishing into a high dimness. A splendid marble floor. Altar steps broad and gracious. Everything on a palatial scale.

I'd done some reading in my guidebook about Spitalfields. When the Wisemans wed there (if they did), it was the centre of the highly skilled silk-weaving trade, and was relatively affluent. Marriage to Jane Middleton might have been a small step up in the world for Wiseman, as the family story suggested. Perhaps it wasn't a love match, but a cold-blooded bit of self-improvement.

It might make sense of a wife being pushed down the stairs thirty years later.

In the year 2000 it looked as though prosperity had come and gone in Spitalfields several times. In some streets it was on its way back. Narrow old houses with wooden shutters and many-paned windows were being gentrified, front doors gleaming with fresh paint.

But in other streets there were glimpses of squalor. Crooked cobbled alleys where the light from the sky didn't reach the ground. The slots of houses all pushed together. How cold the light must be in their small mean rooms. Everywhere I looked I saw windows mended with cardboard, piles of rubbish, black fibrous muck heaped against walls.

This wasn't tourist territory. These poky streets were

jammed with trucks loading and unloading, Indian men standing outside shops, teenage boys slim in tunic and pants trotting along the footpaths with clothes on hangers. Where workers once went blind weaving silk, the sweatshops of the garment trade now churned out cheap clothes for the markets in Brick Lane.

I was feeling conspicuous. Men in doorways wearing Nehru jackets and Astrakhan caps stared. A boy pulling a rack of gaudy dresses across the road watched me all the way to the other side, his head turning so he wouldn't lose sight of me. Was I the only woman out on the street?

Up ahead of me I saw a pale stunted man, his face mauled by some kind of blistered rash, sidle up to a big black man. As I passed I glimpsed the gold watch laid out on the pale man's palm.

'What you looking at, man?' I heard the black man ask.

The man with the rash came back quick as a whip. 'Seven quid.'

Under the viaduct of the railway, the arched vaults were crammed with piles of stuff: broken toilet-pans, mattress-springs, seatless chairs, car steering-wheels. Everything was worn-out, broken, dirty, unrecognisable as a useful object, compacted into a dense mass: no longer individual items but essence of rubbish.

Yet a man stood there selling things, watching as people picked over the piles, as if they might steal something. Taking money for a handful of rusted nails, giving change out of a leather bag hanging from his belt.

In the romantically named Cygnet Lane—a rubbish-strewn passageway between dark weeping brick walls—worn women in saris held out packets of cigarettes. They were listless, hopeless, their skins chalky, their faces blank. One slumped on a milk crate, the packet of cigarettes dangling from her hand, staring at the gutter, too worn out even to try to make a sale.

Or were the cigarettes a front, a code—were these women prostitutes?

This was nothing picturesque. This was real, grinding, fearful poverty. These back lanes of Spitalfields were a living museum of the world Wiseman would have known, a world in which a handful of rusty nails was a saleable commodity. This—the ugly face of the first generation of migrants clinging to a big city—was teaching me more about Wiseman than any amount of dawdling about on the banks of the Thames picking up pieces of roof tile.

Next day I made another early start and went south of the river instead of north. Wiseman had married in Spitalfields, but according to the Mormons his son had been baptised at the church of St Mary Magdalene in Bermondsey, and the address of the parents was Butler's Buildings.

I took the Tube to London Bridge and walked down Borough High Street, past cobbled alleyways and courtyards and along the side of the high brick wall of Marshalsea Prison, where Dickens' father was incarcerated for debt. Right beside that wall was the Southwark Local History Library. I was hoping someone there could locate Butler's Buildings for me.

They couldn't, but they found me a copy of an eighteenth-century map and a magnifying glass. Eventually I located Butler's Buildings, a long thin street with a kink halfway down. The map showed the buildings, too: nineteen houses in an unbroken row down one side of the street, seventeen on the other. On one side of the street, the houses backed straight onto those in the next street over.

Peering at the map, I was starting to smell the Bermondsey of Wiseman's time. 'Mr Choubert's Tannery.' 'Mr Pott's Glue Manufactory.' 'White's Fellmongers.'

How did they breathe?

Putting my *A to Z* alongside the old map, I worked out that Butler's Buildings was now a street called Brunswick Court, a five-minute walk from the river.

By the time the map had given up its secrets I was looking anxiously at my watch. The group of writers had to talk to journalists in the afternoon, and then we were to do a reading at the South Bank. I needed to get back to the hotel. I was cutting things fine. But I was determined to see Brunswick Court.

It had turned into a sultry day by this time, the sunlight grey and unpleasantly hot. Brunswick Court began as a spooky archway under the railway, scabs of black ooze hardened on the bricks. There was nothing old here—Bermondsey was comprehensively bombed during the Blitz—but nothing had really changed either. What had once been Butler's Buildings was still a mean little street, barely wide enough for a car. Where the boxes of terraced houses had lined up next to each other in the eighteenth century there were still small identical houses—though of postwar stained pale brick—squashed up together. On one side the looming brick bulk of Jones Maltings filled the sky and cut off the sun. The sweet reek of the brewery filled the street. The cramped houses on one side, the towering walls of the brewery on the other, pressed in on me.

If Wiseman had been an honest waterman, or a better thief, some genetic variant of me would have grown up somewhere like this, breathing the stink of the brewery in my dreams.

The other end of the street, where the old map showed Bermondsey Workhouse, was now a triangle of park with worn-out grass, and a bit further along was the church of St Mary Magdalene, where the first child of Solomon and Jane Wiseman had perhaps been baptised.

The church was locked. So was the rectory next door, but my eye was caught by a sign on the front door: 'PLEASE DO NOT RING THE DOOR BELL for food before you have read the notice in the window on the right.' The notice in the window on the right read: 'Sorry, no food parcels available until further notice.'

As at Spitalfields, I was in another world, where people were hopelessly, unfixably poor. Wiseman's world.

St Mary Magdalene, all those christenings—but, with that name, wasn't he Jewish? The family story said nothing about it, so I'd always wondered. But people had always looked at me strangely when I tried to voice my doubts. *She's wondering if Solomon Wiseman is Jewish?* I'd see them think. *Is the Pope Catholic?*

Back at the hotel I was getting ready for the reading—the blue or the black? the jacket or the shawl?—when the phone rang. It was a researcher from the Jewish Genealogical Society of Great Britain, whom I'd asked earlier for information about Solomon Wiseman, born 1777. They had no record of him, and the researcher thought he probably wasn't Jewish. He explained that an English Jew called Wiseman would have been descended from German Jews called Weissmann, and most German Jews didn't arrive in England until the early nineteenth century.

'He was probably from Essex originally,' the researcher suggested. 'Essex is full of Wisemans. English Wisemans,' he emphasised. 'The name comes from wyse mann.'

'I see,' I said. 'Thank you. You've been very thorough. Much appreciated.'

I hung up and sat on the bed. I was disappointed. Why? Part of my image of Wiseman, and of myself, had always been coloured by the possibility of Jewishness. Now something was having to shift. Why was I resisting it?

We did the readings, we did the interviews, we had our photographs taken for the paper. The Centenary of Federation was properly celebrated. Then it was all over. One by one the writers and musicians and dancers trundled their suitcases out of the hotel and headed home.

Melissa and I had breakfast together on the last morning.

'So what have you found out about your ancestor?' she asked.

Not much, was one kind of answer. I'd seen the street where he lived, stood on the spot where he was caught stealing. But I still didn't know who he was—what kind of person he might have been. I didn't know whether he stole out of hunger or greed, whether he married for love or money.

Everything, was another kind of answer. What I knew now was simple but important: how inadequate the story about him was. Over the last two weeks he'd burst right out of the membrane of that family tale. I knew him now as a human being, complicated and contradictory. He'd stood and walked and talked, been cold and wet, warm and dry, hungry and full. I couldn't see him, didn't know him, but that didn't matter: what I knew was that he was real. Much more real than *Solomon Wiseman was born in London and worked on the docks.*

A real man had sailed up the Hawkesbury and picked out a hundred acres for himself. A real man had *taken up*, or *taken*, a piece of someone else's place. Not just a story. Something that had really happened.

I was finding it hard to put into words, but I gave Melissa some kind of answer.

She nodded. 'So did he turn out to be Jewish in the end?'

'Ah well,' I said, and explained. 'I'm a bit disappointed,' I added, and heard myself laugh. 'Don't know why.'

'Well,' Melissa said. 'If he was Jewish, that would make him just that much less white.'

As the jumbo heeled in the sky over London, pointing towards home, I rested my forehead against the window and stared down. There was the Thames, drawing its wandering line. There were the hazy spires and roofs, the streets and parks. Wiseman had known them, and I knew them too now.

What I'd discovered here wasn't so much my roots, but the feeling of having roots to discover. It had taken this foreign place—London—to show me the power of belonging. Here, as never before, I could think: this is where my family was from.

But I knew I hadn't finished with my great-great-great grandfather. I'd felt him in Christ Church Spitalfields and I'd felt him in Brunswick Court, Bermondsey. Now I needed to feel him in the place that was home. I had to make the connection: his life, my life, and the place where they came together.

10

Wiseman's Life

I knew I wanted to go on looking for my great-great-great grandfather, and most of all to go again to his house at Wiseman's Ferry. What I'd learned in London about finding the past in the landscape of the present could be applied to that half-remembered place, too.

But daily life enclosed me like a glove when I returned from London and I couldn't get out of the city for some months. It was frustrating until I realised that something else was happening. It began to dawn on me that the Sydney I was walking in now was a different city from the one I'd left only a few weeks before. It was still the city I'd grown up in, where I had lived for most of my life. But now I was seeing it as Wiseman's place as well.

I knew a bit about its past. Third Class at North Sydney Demonstration School had been taken to various historical landmarks: Sydney Cove, where the First Fleet dropped anchor in 1788: eleven ships, around seven hundred convicts and a couple of hundred soldiers to guard them.

We'd seen the area called The Rocks, on the western side of Sydney Cove, where the convicts had lived in caves until there were huts for them. It was all souvenir shops now, but still steep, full of strange tilting dogleg alleys that ended in flights of stone steps.

We'd been taken along Pitt Street and George Street, streets of skyscrapers and brisk men in dark suits. Somewhere under the bitumen, we were told, the invisible Tank Stream still ran. That stream was the reason why Captain Phillip had ordered those eleven ships to come to rest in this cove. There was nothing to see, but we ticked the box on our Excursion Sheet: *Tank Stream*.

We drew pictures of Cadman's Cottage, the oldest building in Sydney; of the anchor of the *Sirius*, flagship of the First Fleet, on its plinth beneath the office blocks; took turns in the seat-shaped stone where the governor's wife had liked to sit in the evening on the headland beside the Botanical Gardens.

It was all a bit like Mum's stories: too close to home to be interesting, too often told, too remote from anything to do with us.

One day in August 2000 I had a free afternoon. I decided to go back to the Mitchell Library and make a start in the archives for anything else about Wiseman. I went by ferry because it was convenient: by coincidence, it was called the *Sirius*. It chugged past Goat Island, past Lavender Bay and beneath the sinister shadowed underside of the Harbour

Bridge, then turned a corner in the water and there I was, right in the middle of Sydney Cove: the Opera House on the left, The Rocks on the right, and Circular Quay ahead.

Nothing was as it had been in 1788. And yet nothing had changed. The narrow cove of green water chopped and sparkled under the sun. With a shock I saw how much like the Thames it was: the same width across the cove, the same wash and smack of water against the shore. And the gulls! Like the ones I'd heard at Three Cranes Wharf, that sad mewing again.

The low spit of land on my left pointed into the main body of the Harbour. With my new eyes I could erase the Opera House and the fancy apartments and see it again as a long rocky arm protecting the cove. Ahead of me, the bay had been squared off to accommodate the wharves, but the shape of the land was still there. I could see the dish of the valley sloping up steeply left and right and running all the way back to where Central Station was now. I could imagine the creek—the Tank Stream—winding down the valley to the bay. Scattered along its banks were tents, huts, a few buildings like Cadman's Cottage, with sagging rooflines and windows that weren't straight.

This was the place Wiseman had been. The Sydney Harbour Ferry *Sirius* was idling, waiting for a spot at Wharf 5, near where the *Alexander* would have dropped anchor with Wiseman on board. They'd have brought the convicts up out of the dark hold—how painfully bright the light must have been! Over to my right, where the cruise ships tied up now, he would have stepped ashore, and glanced up, as I did, at the high ridge of The Rocks. The Harbour Bridge loomed above the whole place now, heroic and overwhelming, but he would have seen the steep hillside, with its angled plates and shelves of rock. He'd have seen the creek, the tents, the raggedy dirt tracks that were about to be named Pitt Street and George Street.

And, up there on the ridge, he might have seen the silhouette of another man, watching.

It was all gone, but it was all here. It had taken a foreign place to let me see what lay underneath my own.

In the library it felt different, too. The Public Record Office in Kew had shown me the power that a piece of paper could hold. It had shown me, too, not to be frightened of those arcane catalogues. I needed help with them, but that was okay. Kew had taught me humility as well.

The librarians walked me through all the catalogues: the Mitchell Library MSS Index Catalogue; the Mitchell Library Leaf Catalogues One and Two; the Sir William Dixson Library MSS Catalogue, including the Archival Estrays and the Supplementary MSS Catalogue; the Contents Lists of MSS Collections and the Small Pictures File. They explained about Webcat and Picman.

The Old Bailey transcripts, in their white boxes on the open shelves, had been beginner's luck.

As my folders filled with Wiseman references—letters, petitions, lists—I was determined to keep things organised. I drew neat headings, made an index of references with circled numbers in colour-coded pens, wrote down all the call numbers, filed away my Request Slip carbons. I was discovering in myself an obsessive I'd never known was there.

I found dozens of references to Wiseman and slowly pieced

together a life for him in Sydney.

He was sentenced in October 1805, sailed on the *Alexander* in January 1806, and arrived in Australia in September of that year. His wife Jane and the four-year-old William came out on the same boat as free settlers. (This wasn't as unusual an arrangement as it sounds. The ratio of men to women in the colony resulted in a fair amount of what the authorities called 'unnatural acts'. From time to time official policy was to increase the number of women, and allowing spouses to emigrate was an efficient way of doing that.)

The first mention of Wiseman after his arrival was in a list of prisoners granted their tickets-of-leave (a kind of parole) in 1810, followed in February 1812 by an Absolute Pardon.

I scratched out a little tally on my notepad, adding up how long he'd been a convict. Six years and six months. Not bad for someone who was to be punished for the term of his natural life—although a long stretch for stealing some timber.

Over the next twenty-five years Wiseman produced a mass of documents, mostly petitions to the governor (whose permission was needed for most things) and business correspondence. I was puzzled, because I'd always got from Mum the idea of him being illiterate. One of the documents explained it: he employed a clerk who lived as part of his household and, according to one account, was 'in a permanent state of inebriety'.

The documents showed the path from penniless convict to wealthy landowner over a period of ten years. He began with an inn and became the owner of two boats in which he traded up and down the coast. Then his boats went further afield to New Zealand for the lucrative seal trade.

Meanwhile Jane Wiseman was having babies. Between 1806 and 1816 she gave birth to five more children—an average of a baby every two years. I was curious about Jane. Had she come willingly to Australia with Solomon? Or was it a matter of choosing between the streets or the workhouse, and going aboard the *Alexander*? What was it like for her, caring for a brood of infants in a settlement of hovels and huts?

But my curiosity had nothing to work on. Beyond the record of the children's births, Jane was mentioned in the documents only once: in a begging petition of 1817 to the Governor she was described as being 'in an actual state of invalidity'.

No wonder, with five children under ten to care for.

All these records were on microfilm, in tidy clerk's copper-plate. Then I filled out yet another request slip: Promissory Notes 1814/1815, AW47, expecting another white box of microfilm. What came back was a brown folder holding three flimsy slips of paper. They were printed, with spaces where you filled in the blanks. The first was dated October 15, 1814:

Four months after date I promise to repay Alexr Riley Esq, or order the Sum of Three Hundred and Sixty-One pounds, Nine shillings and Five pence Sterling.
Solomon Wiseman.

The signature was a compressed squiggle, a shape like a spring lying on its side. The ink was faded, like those I'd seen at Kew, pale brown on the yellowed old paper. But Wiseman's hand had held the pen that made those marks. His hand had taken this piece of paper from someone, Alexander Riley perhaps, laid it on the table, steadied it while he inscribed the shape he'd learned, picked it up and given it back to Riley.

I wanted to rush over to the librarian, his head in the card catalogue. *Look!* I wanted to shout. *His signature! He held this piece of paper in his hand!*

There were three of these Promissory Notes, totalling around six hundred pounds. I guessed that was a massive sum for someone in his position.

Around the same time, I learned from another document, he mortgaged his inn. This was a man taking a big financial risk.

In 1817 he was unable to redeem the mortgage on the inn and had to surrender it. Of his debt to Alexander Riley I could find no record. Around the same time he was granted 200 acres of land on the Hawkesbury. Against this entry, the record noted 'he has recently sustained great loss'.

I read on, hoping to find out what had happened.

He settled on that land and built what he described as a 'farmhouse'. He went on trading up and down the river, carrying other people's crops to the store in Sydney. Each year he applied for convict servants—every settler's source of free labour—and was usually granted half the number he'd asked for. His farm flourished—his speciality was 'hogs' for the salt pork trade. When construction on the Great North Road began, running right past his land, he supplied the lucrative government tender to 'victual the convicts' who were building the road.

But why had he moved to the Hawkesbury? What had happened with the mortgage and all that money he'd borrowed?

The answer came when I went to the *Sydney Gazette*, Sydney's first newspaper. In 1817 it reported that both of Wiseman's boats—trading up and down the coast—were wrecked, within three months of each other. They were his main source of income. With them gone, he had no hope of repaying Alexander Riley or discharging the mortgage on the inn. Whether to escape his debt or simply to start again, he settled on the Hawkesbury.

In 1821 Jane Wiseman died 'after a lingering illness'. She was about forty-five years old. I scoured the records for the slightest hint that her illness might have lingered because she was pushed down the stairs by her husband. I would have loved to find some tiny thread to start tugging on—all those petitions and letters about importing this, that and the other weren't especially dramatic. But there were no clues.

A year after Jane's death, in 1822, Wiseman married the widow of one of his farm-workers, a man named William Warner. His bride's name was Sophia. Now the obsessive-compulsive researcher, I went back to the Old Bailey records and found the trial of a William Warner—perhaps the same one, perhaps not—at about the right time. Like Wiseman, Warner had been a Thames lighterman and had stolen some timber.

Wiseman could have known Warner back in London. It made me wonder if he had known Sophia then, too.

In spite of the lesson I thought I'd learned from all those scrawled family trees I'd dreamed up, I found myself leaping to fill in the blanks. Wiseman grows up knowing Sophia. He comes to love her and plans to marry her. But he's tempted by Jane and she falls pregnant. He has to marry her, even though he's still an apprentice. Sophia marries William Warner and comes out to Australia with him when he's transported. Warner comes to work for Wiseman. Sophia is with him and the childhood romance is rekindled. There's an argument with Jane, who's jealous. She falls down the stairs. Warner conveniently dies too. Wiseman and Sophia marry and live happily ever after. I had to remind myself that, although this was a good story, that's all it was: a story I'd made up out of almost nothing.

After their marriage, Wiseman and Sophia built an extension on their house and called the place Cobham Hall, the name of a stately home in Kent. The section of the river where they lived was known as The Branch, because the first branch or tributary of the Hawkesbury joined the main river at that point. There they lived grandly and entertained the gentry, including—according to the *Gazette*—the governor himself.

Right at the end of my list of references from the catalogues was one just called 'Wiseman, S., MLMSS 3795'. I filled out the request slip without much interest—probably another business letter.

On the contrary, MLMSS 3795 was the only personal letter from Wiseman that I unearthed. It was written in 1828, when he was rich and respectable, to Sophia's brother in England. I gulped it down.

Lower Branch, Hawkesbury, New South Wales
22nd May 1828

Dear Sir and brother,
I have now the unbound pleasure to inform you that I have married your sister Sophia Widow of the late Mr Wm Warner, our marriage took place about two years after the death of her late husband, and since our Union I have learnt to feel her inestimable value, and must acknowledge she is a Woman of Sound Sense, Prudence, and reflection, of a mild temper and accomplishments—therefore to all her relatives I wish to pay a due attention and respected regard as I sincerely feel it the happiest moment of my life,

and am daily raising from threatning pain (by continual losses) into affluence and increased wealth, and my future expectations in life, I trust through Divine Providence will never more be blithed especially as I am joined to a Woman capable of having an opinion of her own; and if agreeable to you I shall correspond at convenient opportunity with you by letter as it is my intention to visit England in the course of 3 years—There was a Captain Pierce who came to this colony about 12 months ago, with a letter to my wife, but did not see the gentleman, nor receive the letter untill after he had sailed from Port Jackson when I was given to understand that such a person had arrived; I did without delay despatch a Couple of Horses to Sydney, in order to convey himself and another gentleman to my residence, but the Ship had left the harbour, the distance from Sydney to my place of abode is 60 miles, and, but 1 mile within these few months almost impassible, at present, Government has several working gangs, called road making parties employed making high roads in that direction, and I victual them by <u>Contract</u>.

To give a candid description of this Colony ('infant' as it is), its surprising rise and progress, would exceed the limits of my present correspondence, suffice to say its a wholesome climate, and every individual may, if his inclinations lead him towards industry, obtain a livelihood—and when infirmities—decease, and incripid old age incapacitates them from industrious earnings, there is an Assylum for them, let their conduct be ever so imprudent or mischievous—christian humanity is become the prevailing <u>motto</u>—Dear Sir I cannot conclude this letter without once more mentioning your sister, she has a conjugal and maternal heart, she is a <u>Wife</u> and a <u>Mother</u> continually preparing the way for my childrens independence and respectability, by teaching temperance and frugality, so to all her relations I beg leave with heartfelt affection to be remembered.

I remain yours with firm affection,
Solomon Wiseman

I found myself feeling sorry for him: the grovelling tone to his brother-in-law, the straining after the grand phrase, the elaborate strings of sentences! The way he betrayed himself at every turn—the words not quite right, the sentences trailing along with no grammar to hold them together, the innocent vulgarity (what gentleman would admit that he 'victualled the convicts by contract'?).

And what did he really think about Sophia? 'Sound sense, mild temper and accomplishments' sounded cold-blooded, as if he might have wanted nothing more than a housekeeper and child-minder. But was there the flicker of another kind of feeling, more heartfelt, in 'I feel it to be the happiest moment of my life'? And what about his appreciation of Sophia being 'capable of having an opinion of her own'? What sort of relationship did that suggest? What sort of man?

The letter might have been what every 'family historian' longs for, to understand their ancestor. But it was also a mass of possibles, maybes, perhapses, as every other document had been.

Whatever the words meant, though, they were his. In two hundred years, the email I wrote yesterday might be hard to interpret too. Human beings were slipperier than the ones I was familiar with on the page: the creatures of fiction. This was the muddle of real life.

In 1838, at the age of sixty, Wiseman died. The obituary that Mum had mentioned was indeed flowery, describing him as 'a very old Colonist, much respected by all the old hands of the Colony as a warm-hearted industrious man'.

Now that I'd read the letter to his brother-in-law, I went back through some of the business correspondence, and found that there, too, I could sometimes hear his tone of voice. This letter was written in 1828:

I am at present awkwardly situated, my stable is left in an unfinished state—the carpenter whom I employed has decamped and like all the other scoundrels of his description who leave their employers when they get in their debt, so did he after getting in mine—he is a free man therefore I shall take out a warrant for his apprehension if I can possibly trace him out. As I am suffering a serious inconvenience by the fellow leaving my stable unfinished, I humbly beg leave to intrude on your kind intercession that I may be allowed a carpenter for the space of three months from Government.

Whatever else he was, Wiseman was no shrinking violet. I was struck by how often he was in the position of defending himself against various kinds of accusations: of defrauding the government, bribing officials, supplying rotten food to the convicts on the road-gangs, of not looking after his assigned servants properly. He always had an answer:

I never received a fortnight's service from that man he was always sick and when sent back from the hospital he told me he was then not able to work and I immediately returned him to Government so I consider Sir the slops I gave him were more than his due...no servants in the colony are better fed and clothed than mine and they are the only men in the neighbourhood that attend divine service with a clean and decent appearance.

Wiseman had a long and difficult relationship with Percy Simpson, the local magistrate. Wiseman's son, who lived not far away in Wollombi, was accused of stealing a horse, and Solomon was forced to appear in court to give evidence:

Mr Wiseman said that the mare belonged to a damned scoundrel who had spread a report that his (Mr Wiseman's) son had stolen a mare belonging to him and had her in the Wollombi—that he had told the man where to go and get the mare and then rushing out of Court in a violent manner giving a most contemptuous look at the magistrate said that if he had known what business he was sent for, he would not have come...

The magistrate admonished him for the contemptuous manner in which he treated the Court...Mr Wiseman again interrupted the court in a rude and violent manner by saying 'I won't stand here listening to your nonsense'... adding that he never affronted a gentleman in his life, he had been 25 years in the Colony but a gentleman he had never affronted. The Magistrate said your conduct to me now on the bench has been most insulting. Mr Wiseman replied I never insulted a gentleman. No! A gentleman I never insult.

I was starting to get a feel for him. Irascible, defensive, unyielding. An entrepreneur who was confident of his own power in the situation, ruthless in using it. And with a snobbery that distinguished between a real 'gentleman' and a pretender.

Percy Simpson was foolish to take on Wiseman—had he forgotten that Wiseman was his landlord? A long correspondence ensued—accusation and counter-accusation—over rent not paid and expiry of the lease. In the end Wiseman insisted that Simpson leave his premises but when the magistrate, who had a large family of young children and an invalid wife, begged for more time, Wiseman relented:

In consideration of the delicate state of health of your Lady Wife and your purse, and young family, children, servants etc as I would not be thought capable of turning you out under the heavens...it being impossible to procure even a shed in this neighbourhood for any amount of money, that I am happy to take an opportunity of saying you may remain in your present residence without rent until the month of May…by which period you must be provided with other quarters.

Was it that he didn't want people to *think* he was capable of turning someone out 'under the heavens'? Or was he genuinely sympathetic? Did he remember at such moments what it had been like in Butler's Buildings, in that life where no one would help you?

I pored over their exchange. I could hear Percy Simpson clearly: vain, self-important, a windbag. But Wiseman swam in and out of focus, now a good man, now a bad one. Now an innocent man unjustly accused, now a scoundrel.

What did others make of him? The Reverend Thomas Atkins' parish included Wiseman's place. Atkins described him as 'a notorious emancipist, self-designated The King of the Branch…Solomon Wiseman, although illiterate, was a man of considerable natural ability, and deeply read in the corruption of human nature.'

I found myself catching fire with indignation. 'Notorious'? 'Deeply read in the corruption of human nature'? How dare this pipsqueak say that!

Then I learned that Atkins had swallowed a glamorised version of Wiseman's crime: a story that he was transported for smuggling on the shores of Dover rather than pinching timber on the muddy old Thames.

Justice Roger Therry, on his circuit, also visited Wiseman,

and took a kindlier view of him as: 'a person of great natural shrewdness and of considerable prosperity; for he was then engaged in the fifth year of a contract with Government, for supplying provisions to convicts who worked upon the roads, that brought him a net income of from £3000 to £4000 a year'. Therry also believed the smuggling story, but added, 'in the Colony his conduct was industrious, and his character for probity irreproachable'.

But my hackles rose again when the judge took the opportunity to have a bit of fun at Wiseman's expense:

In literary attainments of any kind old Solomon was sadly deficient…He condoled with General Darling, who paid a visit to his beautiful place, by informing him frankly that his Excellency, by his measures, had lost all his *population* (meaning popularity) in the district. On inquiring from him the name of a curious bird that attracted Archbishop Polding's attention, Solomon replied—'Your Grace, we call that the laughing jackass in this country, but I don't know the *botanical* name of the bird.' The climax of his intelligence was, however, crowned by another reply he made to Dr Polding. Solomon attached this meaning to the words 'Protestants and Romanists', that the former were Englishmen, and the latter either denizens of Rome or descendants from Romans who had early emigrated to England. With this impression, and in the belief that the Catholic Archbishop was *a Roman*, he said—'I am very sorry to tell your Grace that there's a great down upon the Romans in this country.' 'I don't think so,' said his Grace (thinking of course that Solomon meant the Roman Catholic portion of the community). 'I have received great kindness,' his Grace added, 'from persons of all religious denominations here.' 'Oh my Lord, 'tis a fact, I assure you. There's a great down upon the Romans.' 'And why should there be?' inquired his Grace. 'Because, my Lord, the English people never will forgive Julius Caesar and the Romans for invading their country.' After this answer the Archbishop was dumbfounded, and quite incapable of further discussing the topic with so erudite a critic of historical events.

How dare this silvertail, with his nice education paid for by Daddy, mock a man who'd had to drag himself up by his own bootstraps?

But this exchange made me wonder about Wiseman and his attitude towards the Aboriginal people. If he'd been thinking about the Romans invading Britain, did he draw a parallel with what he himself was doing?

Another account described Wiseman without judging him. It was written by Baron Charles von Hugel, a German botanist, diplomat and army officer:

I was anxious to meet Old Wiseman, but did not know quite how to set about it. He was known to be most hospitable to people he knew, but rather eccentric with strangers, as I was told by Capt. McCumming. However, chance favoured me. As I approached the house, I found a number of men standing there together and, when I came up to them, I asked after Crawford's Inn. An elderly man pointed the way, but added: 'You seem to be a stranger in these parts; if you care to accept the hospitality of my house, I would be able to make you more comfortable there after a long day's journey.' I thanked him and accepted, and asked whether I had the pleasure of speaking to Mr Wiseman. He confirmed this and asked me whether I were not the Baron who had come on the *Alligator*, and I confirmed this...

After the meal, Old Wiseman came back and asked me if I required anything further. I answered him, nothing whatsoever, except that, if it did not keep him away from some other better entertainment, I would appreciate his company. Sit down, I said, and let us talk a little about the colony. The old man stood still for a moment, then he said: 'You are a stranger, I would not like to deceive you. I am an emancipist.' 'I know that,' I replied. 'I knew that when I came into your home, and when I accept a man's hospitality, his company must needs be agreeable to me too.'

Wiseman: Not everyone thinks as you do. A lot of people are pleased to accept Old Wiseman's comfortable rooms and stay a few days in this beautiful district, but avoid and despise Wiseman himself.

Myself: I can't believe that. You are probably imagining things. I know your house is a favourite place for young couples to spend their honeymoon.

Wiseman: Yes, one couple spent their honeymoon here—Mr [Deas] Thomson after he married Miss Bourke... I arranged an apartment for him in my house as best I could and, on the day of the marriage, he arrived here in the evening. But we can't really speak very highly about the way in which our hospitality was received. The young wife did not address a single word to us during her whole stay here, and when they left, and Mrs Wiseman wished her a pleasant journey, she turned her head away without replying and did not even wave as they drove away...

I could cite a number of other instances of this kind...

and I therefore keep my children away when I have reason to fear a humiliation for them. You must pardon me (he said with deep emotion) if perhaps I do not use the right words or am less polite to you than I should be. But I am a seaman and paid little attention to fine manners in my youth, and you don't learn them here.

Ah! This was another Wiseman, a man of sensitivity, of feeling, and those contradictory images started to come into focus. So much made sense now: his quickness to anger, his defensiveness, his single-minded pursuit of wealth. This was a man who—day after day, year after year—had to deal with the humiliation of being despised as an 'emancipist' and mocked by the likes of Atkins and Therry. This was a man who, even though he had made good on the other side of the world, could not escape the English class system. I warmed to the Baron for treating Wiseman with courtesy, and for leaving such a long and vivid account of him for me to read.

There were two more things to see: a picture of Wiseman, and one of his house. I'd put off looking at them. I somehow wanted to come at them in a roundabout way. I wanted to know everything else before I met Wiseman face to face. I chose to look at them in private, at home on the internet, rather than in the library.

I was pleased that a portrait of Wiseman had survived. It was more than I'd have hoped for. But, sitting in my workroom listening to a child go past on a squeaky tricycle beyond the hedge, waiting for the image to appear on the screen, I was apprehensive.

I'd had the experience in my twenties, when I was researching a film project about consumer protection, of being asked by a businessman how much a new Holden Commodore cost. It was a test: he knew I wouldn't know. I'd stammered out some ludicrous figure. There I was, calling myself a writer, trying to do a film about consumers, and I didn't know the first thing.

I had a feeling Wiseman would have been like that. Tough, shrewd, worldly, aggressive—he'd have eaten me for breakfast. He'd despise my soft-handed life, twittering around putting a word here, a word there, making little stories about not very much.

When the image popped out onto the screen it gave me a fright. He was standing at a table, looking directly at me. A telescope rested along one hand. The fingers of the other were interleaved in the pages of a book. He was wearing a dark tailored coat, a white shirt with a high collar, some kind of dark bow at the neck.

And the face—big, powerful, pronounced chin, tight-held mouth. The force of his will! He came right out of the picture, dominating, unyielding. Eyeing the painter as if to say, *Don't muck around with me, mate.*

It was a spooky feeling to be looking him right in the face. Almost more real than I could handle. He frightened me.

Then the house: 'Wiseman's villa', circa 1835, unknown artist, watercolour.

The top half of the picture was filled with a high ridge of rocks and grass with a few scattered shrubs, all soft greens, soft browns, a landscape of wash and daub. The bottom half showed a formal garden, surrounded by a stone wall higher than a person. And, slap bang in the middle, a two-storeyed house that must have been drawn with a ruler: severe, symmetrical, floating in the soft blur of the hill behind it.

Thames lighterman turned gentleman. The book is a nice touch for a man who couldn't read.

The picture was full of details that said *I am rich:* some high-stepping fine-boned horses, a line of fat cows, yards full of pigs, workers doing various things with all this livestock, a couple of carriages coming down the hill.

A woman in a long blue dress was walking in the garden. If the picture was done in 1835, this was Sophia.

And when I peered closely I could make out a man in a blue coat sitting on the verandah, taking his ease, legs apart, a servant bending over him: Mr Wiseman, new-hatched gentleman, lord of all he surveyed.

After all this research I was the world authority on Solomon Wiseman. Whatever he'd left behind to prove that he once lived on the earth, I'd found.

But my work didn't seem finished. I felt I'd hardly started.

Was it because I needed to know more about Wiseman? How much more? I wondered what it would take for me to feel I had enough. Was there any way a search like this would ever end? Or would finding out more and more about Solomon Wiseman become a hobby, compulsive but useless?

A whole other part of the story remained hidden, too: the part that was the answer to the question I'd been faced with on the Sydney Harbour Bridge a year earlier. What happened when Wiseman encountered Aboriginal people, up on the piece of land where he'd built that fine stone house?

After four or five months' work in the archives I was no closer to an answer. In the hundreds of pages of documents by and about Wiseman, there was absolute silence on the matter of the original inhabitants.

I'd once asked Mum about the Aboriginal people on the

Wiseman's villa, with its high stone wall, blank back and cleared surrounds.

land that Wiseman *took up*. She said she wasn't sure, but she thought that, by the time Wiseman had arrived there, they'd all gone.

I'd accepted it then without really thinking about it, but now I did the sums. Wiseman went to the Hawkesbury around 1817. That was about three decades after the First Fleet sailed into Sydney Harbour. Was it possible that they'd all gone, already, from a place so remote you could only get to it by boat?

The silence about the Aboriginal people in the documents about Wiseman could have meant anything. It could have meant that they were all gone. Or that they weren't gone, but that nothing happened significant enough to write down. Or that the things that happened were events no one wished to record.

There were no Aboriginal people in 'Wiseman's villa'. Just the house, the horses, the man on the verandah. But beyond Wiseman's high white wall, beyond that almost-bare hillside, was a gesture towards the bush that lay beyond Mr Wiseman's hundred acres. In the picture it was hardly there: a smudge like smoke on the page.

If they'd been anywhere, that's where the Aboriginal people would have been: out there in the bush. I had to move the eyeline along, re-frame the scene. I had to put them back into the picture.

First, though, I needed to see the picture properly: not these smears of watercolour, but the place itself.

12

The Ghost Room

For Wiseman in his boat, the trip to his place would have taken a day or two, depending on weather and tide. Out of Sydney Harbour, along the coast and in at Broken Bay. Then through the gorges of the lower Hawkesbury up as far as the place where the river did a right-angle turn.

For me, in October 2000, it was an hour and a half in the car. The farther out I went, the more garages each house had. After the three-car-garage belt, the retirement villages started. Elmsleigh Gardens. Surrey Manor. Then the market gardens, the orchards, the riding schools.

I knew I'd left the city behind when I passed a pile of bulging bags on the roadside outside a farm with a big handwritten sign: POO $2.50.

All this time the road had been climbing, and now the gardens and orchards gave way to a high dry ridge where bush pressed in against the road, dark-trunked stringybarks and a dense tangle of undergrowth.

What would it be like to visit Wiseman's house after all these years, with glasses on this time?

It seemed I'd been driving forever along the tunnel of trees when the road tilted down and the bush changed, the sombre stringybarks giving way to paler grey gums with gleaming silver skins. Hawkins Lookout, the sign announced. I swung off the road and there it was: the spectacular gorge of the Hawkesbury.

I stood at the lookout, on the edge of a sheer drop. I had to hang onto the railing. I was floating away, lost in this place.

It was a landscape out of a legend, monumental, almost melodramatic, too big for the eye to take in. Way below, the river—half a mile wide—was a gigantic band of khaki, pressing up tight against its banks. It sparkled brown under a slant of sun, a sheet of moody brilliance, and curved majestically between ramparts of rock and bush, almost-vertical escarpments like the one I was standing on, where slabs of sandstone tumbled and frayed down the slope.

I felt I'd travelled to a foreign country. For a moment I even worried that I didn't have the right kind of money.

After it left the lookout, the road coiled down the escarpment in the hairpin bends I remembered from when I was ten. Suddenly I was at the bottom, outside the house that my ancestor built.

Wiseman's villa was still the highest building in the settlement, pressed up against the base of the hill. So naked in the watercolour, it was covered up now, hidden away. Enormous trees smothered the buildings from the street side and additions at the back had obscured the original structure. Behind it, the steep hillside pressed down, overgrown with bush where in the watercolour it was cleared.

But from the front, it was exactly as it was in the painting: the verandahs, looking down to the river, the elegant curved fanlight over the front door and the semicircular stone steps.

A few other buildings clustered on the slope below: the school, a few shops, the post office. Below these buildings was a parched expanse of grass with a concrete cricket pitch and swings. That was where Wiseman's formal garden must have been. Beyond that, a fringe of she-oaks and reeds, and then the river.

And across the river, stupendous cliffs. They seemed to rise straight up out of the water, a wall of rock a couple of miles long, penning in the river and the settlement: the bedrock exposed by the action of the river the way a knife opens up a cake. In places the wind had breached the mouse-grey skin of the sandstone so that the golden flesh beneath was revealed in glowing overhangs and caves. Twisted trees seemed to grow out of rock, their trunks a scribble on the face of the cliff.

I found myself scanning that confusion of rock and shadow, darkness and light, trying to make sense of it. It was like watching the sea: from moment to moment the light fell differently on the recesses and bulges, so that a pattern of gold and grey that I'd seen a moment ago was gone when I looked for it again.

I didn't remember the cliffs from my visit here all those years ago. I remembered Mum standing here exclaiming and pointing, but I hadn't seen a thing.

As if silenced by the solemnity of that wall of rock brooding over it, everything was still in the hamlet below. I turned towards the villa. The sun was heavy across my shoulders, so bright it seemed black.

I was going to take a room at the hotel tonight. Why not? Jane Wiseman might appear and tell me what really happened. I was family, after all.

The publican was doing the books at the bar when I came in. Drinking was mostly what happened in this pub, I could see, and bookish ladies of a certain age weren't the usual customers. He was surprised to be asked for a room.

'It'll be seventy-two dollars,' he said.

'That's fine.'

'There's no ensuite rooms, love.'

'That's okay.'

'No credit cards either, love. It'll have to be cash.'

But this bookish lady was determined. 'That's okay,' I said cheerfully. 'I'm here for the ghost.'

At last he glanced up at me. 'Mrs Wiseman? That'll be Room 9.'

I started to explain about her being my great-great-great grandmother. 'Is it true her ghost appears sometimes?'

I could see him making an effort. I was, after all, prepared to pay seventy-two dollars, cash, for a room with no ensuite.

'Not appears as such,' he said. 'An old lady staying there one time felt something strange. Come down in the morning white as a sheet.'

'What did she see?'

'Oh, just sort of creakings. That kind of thing. Tappings.' He shrugged, then remembered. 'Oh and one time the piano started playing, all by itself.'

Aha, I thought. 'Playing what?'

'Nothing, just noise.'

The room in which Mrs Wiseman tapped and creaked and made an old lady go white as a sheet was small, hemmed in by the trees. Everything was pink except a red-and-orange swirly carpet. Pink walls, darker pink woodwork. Twin beds with pink chenille bedspreads. A pink pressed-tin ceiling.

I'd expected something a little grander. More atmospheric. Less pink. But perhaps it would look better at night.

After nearly two hundred years, the ferry was still the only way across the river. I joined the queue and drove on, scraping the front of the car against the steep ramp.

The tide was turning. The water was dimpled and puckered. As the ferry slid across, a few seagulls came swooping and crying along the river.

I felt my great-great-great grandfather, almost unbearably close. This was his river, his ferry. These cliffs and this bush couldn't have changed shape much in two hundred years. I was hearing what he heard, seeing what he saw.

The ferry docked. As I drove off, the ferry-man in his orange safety vest waved cheerily as if he took me for a local and I waved back. This time I drove off diagonally, the way the locals were doing. No scrape. If things had been different, and Wiseman's younger daughter had stayed near home instead of marrying a man from further north, I'd *be* a local.

I drove around, up the valley of the Macdonald River to the village of St Albans, and then back. I stopped and looked at huts made of vertical slabs of timber, now teetering sideways into the grass, and various old-looking brick cottages. I stopped at every graveyard and looked for the markers that I remembered from my visit here with Mum, but I couldn't find 'Henery'.

The cows were all behind fences now.

After dinner I sat up in bed in Room 9. It was as pink by night as it was by day. I had my notebook and pen at the ready. I looked around, trying to feel receptive to a spirit, but met only the cold grey eye of the TV. Outside a dog was yelping, tied to the verandah post, while its owner was no doubt drinking in the bar beneath me.

Jane Wiseman had six children, I wrote in my notebook, trying to focus my mind. She probably breastfed each one for a year or two, weaned them, and fell pregnant again straight away. She'd have been in a permanent blur of hormones.

By contrast, Wiseman must have been a man of huge energy and drive, with enough power of will to turn his life from disaster to triumph.

If I was honest with myself, I didn't know what I wanted Jane Wiseman to tell me when she appeared at the foot of the bed. And maybe she knew that, because even after I turned out the light she didn't appear. From the bar a murmur of voices floated up and the occasional laugh, possibly at the expense of the lady in Room 9.

The bed, although sagging in the middle, was comfortable. Next thing I knew, it was morning.

Jane may have been nowhere to be found, but her house was still here, so I decided to look around. I found myself in the central hallway, where I'd been with Mum all those years ago. It had begun life as the back of the original house. I peered up, looking for the bricked-over openings of old windows, but it seemed that the place had never had windows at the back or sides.

The door—originally opening onto the yard—was embedded in stone blocks, half a metre thick. It was low-browed, squat, solid as the stones themselves, held in with jambs the size of railway sleepers.

I was visualising the house in the watercolour: a powerful box, with windows only at the front, and this one tunnel-like doorway at the back. Standing there fingering the ancient wood, I realised it was reminding me of the doors of castles I'd seen in Europe. Doors designed to keep people out.

How interesting, I thought: a house with no windows except at the front, overlooking a formal garden in which nothing grew higher than a man's knee. Around it on all sides, a high stone wall. At the back, a hillside cleared of every tree, every bush. And a door that said: *You cannot come in.*

What I was looking at was not just a gentleman's villa. It was a fortress.

Suddenly I was claustrophobic in this dark, tree-shaded building, this whole silent little settlement. At this moment I was absolutely certain—as sure as if I'd seen it with my own eyes—that there'd been trouble here on this quiet bend of the river. It might have been trouble with escaped convicts or bushrangers. But in that moment of seeing the place with new eyes, what I saw were spears and guns, and bright blood soaking into the hot dirt. I imagined this fortress being built so that, if any more blood was spilled, Wiseman could be sure it wouldn't be his.

All gone? I wondered.

13
A Little Learning

Aboriginal people didn't feature much in my Social Studies classes at school. We cut boomerangs out of brown cardboard and painted them with zigzags. We drew *gunyahs* in coloured pencil and learned that a *woomera* was a throwing-stick. You hurled a spear with it. I didn't understand how you threw a spear with a stick, but I drew a long thin brown thing in my book, and it got a gold star.

The Australian history I learned in 1960 was really the history of the explorers, and the Aboriginal people were mostly an adjunct to them. Matthew Flinders, for example, the first man to circumnavigate Australia: Aboriginal people welcomed him and he'd entertained them by cutting their beards and hair. Most of the explorers seemed to have a 'native guide', often called Jacky. Why were the Aboriginal people so helpful? Was it because, as we were taught, they thought that the Europeans were the white ghosts of their own ancestors?

In that case, though, what about those other Aboriginal people, the ones who threw spears at the Europeans and shouted words that meant 'go away'? The explorer Charles Sturt had met a lot of different groups of Aboriginal people as he travelled along the Murray River. Some of them treated him like family, others tried to kill him. He couldn't see any rhyme or reason in it.

Going by what we learned at school, the Aboriginal people had some funny ideas. They had this thing called 'going walk-about', which was part of being a nomad. They went to one place and ate all the food they could find, and then they went off somewhere else and ate all the food there. They didn't build proper houses because they were always going walk-about, and they had to go walkabout because they didn't know about farming. They hunted and gathered, that was all. Two hundred years after Sturt had recorded his puzzlement, our Social Studies textbooks hadn't made much progress in under-standing the first Australians.

Between the lines was the message that they had more or less disappeared. It was sad, but an inevitable consequence of the fact that we were more robust (not dying of measles and the common cold) and more advanced technologically, having guns rather than wooden spears. Darwin had decreed, and how could we argue? The fittest survived.

I'd learned quite a bit since those days in that stuffy class-room at North Sydney Demonstration School. The 1967 Referendum that gave the Aboriginal people the vote, and counted them in the census for the first time, took place when I was seventeen, and that made me do some thinking. *You mean they didn't count as humans before? You mean they weren't allowed to vote?*

Students only a few years ahead of me at university had gone on a 'freedom ride'—modelled on the ones in the segregated states of the USA—to outback towns. I admired them but knew I'd have been too timid to go. In 1988, the sacred national day, Australia Day, which celebrated the landing of the First Fleet, was declared a National Day of Mourning by Aboriginal people, and many of us non-indigenous sympathisers joined them on a march through the streets of Sydney.

But when I tried to fit together the few things I knew about the Aboriginal people with Solomon Wiseman settling on the Hawkesbury, all I got was a confusing static of contradictions.

I needed to get educated.

But how? Perhaps I should meet some Aboriginal people and ask them. But which 'Aboriginal people'? I knew enough by now to know they were not the uniform bloc we'd learned about at school. Should I talk to urban mixed-descent Aboriginal people, like the woman on the Harbour Bridge? Or those I'd seen in documentaries, the people living out among spinifex and red dirt, walking barefoot and killing goannas?

And what was I going to ask? *Please give me a quick lesson on Aboriginal culture?* Or even worse: *Would you mind telling me about the things that my people did to your people?*

That would make me just another whitefeller wanting to get something: not a dot painting dirt cheap, not an authentic boomerang, not even a hundred acres of land, but stories.

I decided to start by doing some homework on my own. I would see what came next.

Walking up from the Quay towards the Mitchell Library one more time, I felt the pinch of the slope in my calves, the November sun hot on my shoulders. Up Phillip Street, past the corner where the first Government House had been. The hill was steep. Wiseman would have felt it in his calves as he walked up here.

As I pushed at one of the grand doors of the library, for perhaps the five hundredth time in my life, I thought to look at them. They were covered with panels of bronze bas reliefs. Scenes from antiquity, I'd always assumed, to go with the fluted stone columns: Diana the huntress with perky little breasts, Apollo with his lyre hiding his rude bits, that kind of thing.

But this time I saw something different from Diana or Apollo. Each panel depicted an Aboriginal subject: *Hunter with Woomera and Spear*; *Lubra with Fishnet*; *Man Making Fire*. They were beautifully made, the people depicted as dignified, strong, skilful, the detail fine and convincing.

Had every generation done this then, from mine all the way back to 1788—tried to find a way to put Aboriginal together with European? The sculptors of these panels—had they been driven, as I was, to acknowledge something?

These images of noble old men with beards, these dignified women staring gravely out at the viewer, must have seemed progressive, even revolutionary when they'd been made. The world they depicted was still called 'primitive', and yet the sculptors had glorified it in bronze, giving it as much value as the classical pediment up above.

Now these images didn't look so progressive. I didn't quite know what to think. It was a long way up from boomerangs on tea towels, but it suggested that the Aboriginal people could be used simply as surface decoration, as exotics, as exhibits out of a museum. As something that was *gone*.

Let this be a warning, I thought, and pushed on into the library.

14
The News of the Day

To ease myself in, and because I didn't know how else to start, I began with the simple stuff: the written record. I was an amateur researcher, but I knew how to find the governors' despatches to their masters in London.

I was good at the nuts and bolts of the Mitchell now. I had a special dollar coin for the lockers that I kept with my reader's ticket. I knew the best spot on the front steps to sit for lunch—on the side, behind the handrail, up against the most easterly column. While I was there I always greeted the ghost of Bea Miles, an eccentric who used to stand on these steps with a sandwich board offering 'Recitations from Shakespeare. Sonnets Threepence, Scenes from a Play One Shilling'.

I started with the first despatches, from 1788, looking

especially for references to the Hawkesbury and the Aboriginal people. It didn't take long to find one. A few months after the First Fleet came to rest in Sydney Harbour, Governor Phillip went back out through the Heads and turned left. A few hours' sailing time north, he found an opening in the coast he called Broken Bay, guessed it was the entrance to a river, and went in to explore.

He was right that it was a river—it was the Hawkesbury. What happened next took place less than thirty kilometres from where Wiseman settled twenty-five years later:

> When the south branch of Broken Bay was first visited we had some difficulty in getting round the headland…having very heavy squalls of wind and rain, and where we attempted to land there was not sufficient water for the boat to approach the rocks, on which were standing an old man and a youth…after pointing out the deepest water for the boats, [they] brought us fire, and going with two of the officers to a cave at some distance, the old man made use of every means in his power to make them go in with him, but they declined; and this was rather unfortunate, for it rained hard and the cave was the next day found to be sufficiently large to have contained us all…
>
> When we returned, two days afterwards…the old man… met us with a dance and song of joy…A hatchet and several presents were made to them, and as I intended to return to Port Jackson the next day every possible means were taken to secure his friendship, but when it was dark he stole a spade, and was caught in the fact. I thought it necessary to show that I was displeased with him, and therefore, when he came to me, pushed him away, and gave him two or

three slight slaps on the shoulder with the open hand, at the same time pointing to the spade. This destroyed our friendship in a moment, and seizing a spear he came close up to me, poised it, and appeared determined to strike; but whether from seeing that his threats were not regarded— for I chose rather to risk the spear than fire on him—or from anything the other natives said who surrounded him, after a few moments he dropped his spear and left us.

I read this again and again, trying to make sense of it. It was so sad and puzzling. Why was the old man so welcoming, why did he dance with joy? If he'd wanted to steal the spade, wouldn't he have been able to do it well enough to avoid being caught? Why didn't he spear Phillip?

I could hear Phillip's voice, but I couldn't hear the old man's. I had a feeling he might have told the story differently.

Only a short time later, back in the settlement, the governor's gamekeeper was speared. No one knew why (or if they did, they weren't telling). This time Phillip sent a party of soldiers out. The captain in charge, Watkin Tench, left this account of his orders:

His Excellency informed me...that we were to proceed to the peninsula at the head of Botany Bay...and thence... to bring away two natives as prisoners; and to put to death ten; that we were to...cut off and bring in the heads of the slain; for which purpose hatchets and bags would be furnished.

No one died on this occasion but it wasn't long before the violence started.

Aboriginal people attacked settlers; settlers and soldiers

attacked back. Not every day, not every week. But on and off, like a headache.

Where these things happened wasn't always specified, but two places were often mentioned: the Nepean River and the Hawkesbury River. Even though I'd lived in Sydney all my life, I realised I was confused about exactly where they were.

The map showed me why. Sydney is on the seaward edge of a natural basin ringed by mountains. When the first European explorers headed south-west, they came across a river that flowed from south to north along the base of these mountains, and called it the Nepean. Other explorers headed north, and came across a river that flowed from west to east. They called it the Hawkesbury. It took them quite some time to realise that these were the same river. In the north-west corner of the basin, the river did an abrupt right-angle turn.

As it happened, the name of the place on that bend was now Wiseman's Ferry.

In addition to flowing in two directions and having two names, the river also had two distinct personalities. The part that lay west of Sydney ran through flat ground, a floodplain of fertile alluvial soil. The part that lay north of Sydney had cut down through a vast sandstone plateau, and ran through a cleft between towering cliffs and buttresses, with only small pockets of good land.

Nothing grew around Sydney itself. (It still doesn't. That was why Mum needed all that cow manure.) The first good farms were on the river west of the township, on those fertile river-flats. Settlers cleared, fenced and planted. Pretty soon the farms were everywhere along the river.

It was these small farms—isolated and vulnerable—that were usually attacked. Soldiers were stationed in the area, but

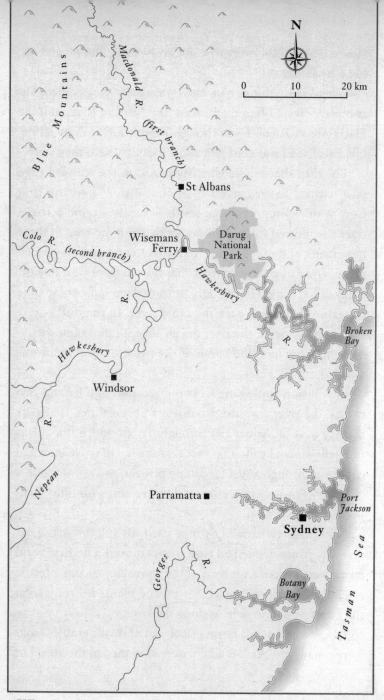

When roads were primitive, wagons slow, and the bush full of robbers, rivers made the best highways.

at harvest time the Aboriginal people swooped in, set fire to field after field of ripe grain, and were gone before the soldiers could get there. Settlers were speared, Aboriginal people were shot.

Sixteen years after Phillip smacked that old man, in December 1804, another governor, John King, tried to deal with the violence on the Hawkesbury:

One of the settlers recently fix'd below Portland Head, who was much annoyed by the natives in June last, delivered me a memorial, said to be signed by all the settlers in that district, requesting they might be allowed to shoot the natives frequenting their grounds, who had threatened to fire their wheat when ripe. On further enquiry I found that none of the settlers had authorised this man to put their signatures to the paper, and that his fears of what might be had operated with him more forcibly than any present or future probability of the natives again being inimical to him or his neighbours...

Wishing to be convinced myself what cause there was for these alarms, three of the natives from that part of the river readily came on being sent for. On questioning the cause of their disagreement with the new settlers they very ingenuously answered that they did not like to be driven from the few places that were left on the banks of the river, where alone they could procure food; that they had gone down the river as the white men took possession of the banks; if they went across white men's grounds the settlers fired upon them and were angry; that if they could retain some places on the lower part of the river they should be satisfied and would not trouble the white men. The observation and request appear to be so just and so equitable that I assured them no more settlements should be made lower down the river.

This was two years before Wiseman arrived in Australia. I was getting warm: Portland Head is only a short distance upstream from Wiseman's Ferry.

In spite of King's promise, settlement on the lower river continued. As far as I could see, no one ever mentioned the governor's promise to the Aboriginal men again. In April 1805, King noted:

I am much concerned to state that, within these Three Weeks past, the Natives have been very troublesome among the distant Settlements at the South Creek and the lower part of the Hawkesbury River...The house belonging to a Settler was set on Fire by...natives. After a search the mangled and burnt Limbs of the Settler and his Man were found, some in the Ashes and others scattered...I directed a party of Military to take post at the Branch and to drive the Natives from thence, first assuring them that if the Murderers were given up all further Resentment should cease.

A few months earlier, King had seemed to understand the Aboriginal point of view. Now he regarded them as a kind of pest and sounded genuinely puzzled that they weren't happy to be dependent on charity: 'Notwithstanding the liberality with which the Settlers supply these people with Corn...to keep on good Terms with them, yet at the period of Maize Harvest no consideration can restrain them from destroying a much greater quantity than they can consume by eating.'

Ten years later the situation had deteriorated. In June 1816 Governor Lachlan Macquarie reported that:

> in consequence of various Subsequent Acts of Atrocity being Committed by the Natives in the remote parts of the Settlements, I found it Necessary to Order Three Detachments on the tenth of April to proceed to those Districts most infested and Annoyed by them giving them instructions to make as many Prisoners as possible; this Service Occupied a Period of 23 days, during which time the Military Parties very rarely met with any of the Hostile Tribes; the Occurrence of most importance which took place was under Captain Wallis's direction, who, having surprized One of the Native Encampments and meeting with some resistance, killed 14 of them and made 5 Prisoners.

Macquarie admitted that 'some few innocent Men, Women and Children may have fallen in these Conflicts', but hoped that 'this unavoidable Result, and the Severity which has attended it, will eventually strike Terror amongst the surviving Tribes, and deter them from the further Commission of such sanguinary Outrages and Barbarities'.

In the same month he proclaimed what amounted to martial law against the Aboriginal people:

> on occasions of any Natives coming armed, or in a hostile Manner without Arms, or in unarmed Parties exceeding Six in Number, to any Farm belonging to or occupied by British Subjects in the Interior, such Natives are first to be desired in a civil Manner to depart from the said Farm, and if they persist in remaining thereon, or attempt to

plunder, rob, or commit any kind of Depredation, they are then to be driven away by Force of Arms by the Settlers themselves.

In other words, for a period from June 1816, settlers could with impunity shoot Aboriginal people more or less on sight.

This was a shock. No one ever told me about this violence on the Hawkesbury, or that it was dealt with in this way.

And Mum's story about the Aboriginal people being all gone by the time Wiseman arrived on the Hawkesbury was looking threadbare. He settled on the river around 1817. Even if he got there after these troubles, it can't have been long after.

Having worked my way through the despatches I turned to the *Sydney Gazette*. Its first issue came out in 1803, three years before Wiseman arrived, and for the next twenty years hardly an issue went by without a piece on the 'black savages'. The tone varied from jocular to indignant. To get a feel for events before Wiseman came to the river, I started at the beginning. Judging by the reports in the *Gazette*, things were pretty busy in June and July of 1804:

among the reaches about Portland Head their ravages have been felt with much greater severity than elsewhere...Last Friday se'nnight the farms of Crumby and Cuddie at the South Creek were totally stripped by a formidable body of natives supposed to be about 150 in number...

Another group made a visit to Tench's River on the *maraud*, where getting among the corn of J. Kennedy without endeavouring to conceal themselves they were speedily discerned *gathering in the crop* with unusual activity: the settler disapproving their diligence as it promised but little advantage to the interests of his own family, instantly embraced the means of repelling a visit that had no real claim upon the laws of hospitality, and by a few discharges obliged them to retire with a trifling booty...

Some short time since, a settler's wife with a large family, entertained half-a-dozen of these idlers with an almost reprehensible hospitality, and they in return, amused her with assurances of their best wishes and gratitude to her bounty, but in the very interim, a body of their colleagues were busily employed in clearing a whole acre of corn, which they carried off either in canoes or on their shoulders.

These things didn't happen to Wiseman, of course, but they'd happened only ten years earlier and a few kilometres from where they *could* have happened to him.

The *Gazette*, meanwhile, was in no doubt how to interpret all this: 'It may verily be advanced, that no set of people in the known world were ever so totally destitute as these are of industry and ingenuity, or whose innate indolence rendered them so wretchedly inattentive to the very means of subsistence.'

Shortly before Wiseman arrived on the river, the *Gazette*'s reports of 'outrages' and 'atrocities' increased: between March and August 1816 they averaged one a month, in various parts of the settlement. After 1816—when Macquarie declared martial law—there were fewer reports for several years. When they resumed, the attacks usually happened further away from

Sydney as the frontier pushed further out.

Squinting at the smudged old print of the *Sydney Gazette*, I was more and more appalled. I'd never known about any of this. Even worse, I'd never thought to ask.

I found nothing about Wiseman here. My original question—'What did he do when he encountered the Aboriginal people?'—still had no clear answer.

But it was becoming less important to fill in the blanks of that specific story. Another story was taking over: the larger one of what happened when white met black on the edge of settlement across the country. If you wanted to put it in one word, you'd say there'd been a war.

When the library closed I walked down Macquarie Street to the old Moore Stairs that ran to the water's edge near the Opera House. This part of the point would have been, before buildings and roads, a kind of tabletop falling away steeply to the harbour. From here I could see the whole bay. Wiseman had been here, yes, but there'd been another bay before he'd arrived, and from the top of Moore Stairs it laid itself out before me, detail by detail.

There'd have been a little beach there in the corner where the creek (the Tank Stream) met the bay, fine yellow sand with a rim of water-smoothed sticks and tiny star-shaped shells at the high-tide mark. Behind that, coarse pale grass and casuarina trees with their needles whistling in the breeze. Embedded in the sand there'd have been rounded boulders slippery with bright seaweed, dotted with periwinkles and oysters. Across the bay the slope would have been honeycombed with overhangs and caves, cold and dank even in the blaze of midday. The whole hillside would have been strewn with gigantic flakes of sandstone, cut-grass growing in the cracks between the rocks.

How did I know? How was it that I could see it, hear it, almost smell it?

Because I'd spent my life knowing this place. In other parts of the harbour, away from the Opera House and Circular Quay, I mucked around in boats through my childhood. I'd slipped on that seaweed that was like brilliant green hair, cut my feet on those oysters, picked off those periwinkles to admire their humbug black-and-white stripes. I'd gone into dank overhangs on other slopes of canted sandstone, felt the chill strike up from the cold rock, ran back out into the sun. I'd discovered thumbnail beaches at the head of coves where runnels of fresh water splashed down and angophoras shook their leaves overhead. I knew this place in my bones.

And this—this paradise of blue water, yellow sand, a cove orientated perfectly to give shelter from the cold winter wind but let in the cooling breeze of summer, a cove with all the fresh water and oysters and fish that a person could need—this was the place where those ships had come in, those strange people stepped ashore and planted their flag and said, *all this is ours now*.

15
Historians

Back in my workroom, books by historians piled up on my desk. As the days of summer wore away, I kept scribbling notes and sorting them in folders.

Within a couple of months of that moment in 1788 when the Union Jack was raised, two men had been speared. As the edge of settlement moved across the country, so did a fire-front of violence that burned well into the twentieth century in the remote parts of northern Australia. There were no big battles, nothing named and famous like the Battle of Little Big Horn. This was a guerrilla war: sparks of violence varying in intensity from place to place. Settlers carried guns and used them frequently, often using the ambiguous word 'disperse' to describe what they were doing. Aboriginal women were kept prisoner by settlers for sexual purposes. Family groups as well as warriors were ambushed and shot or driven over high cliffs. Sometimes they were given flour laced with arsenic. Warning signs were displayed to frighten off attackers: Aboriginal ears nailed to the wall of a hut, an Aboriginal corpse hanging from a tree with a corncob in its mouth.

Settlers were speared and burned in their huts, travellers were ambushed and attacked, settler families on isolated stations were killed—men, women and children.

The historians quoted document after document, from the easily accessed governors' despatches to the most obscure letters and journals deep in the archives. They were a revelation. Here, for example, was a settler lying in his hut at night, convinced that he was about to be attacked:

> all the horrible stories I had ever heard thronged to my recollection...I began to picture to myself the dreary bush outside, and the forms that might even then be creeping up in silence...the perspiration streamed from every pore. My hearing seemed unnaturally sharpened, and the Bush seemed as noisy as it had before been silent: all round the hut I fancied I heard the cracking of dry sticks and the rustling of grass.

A policeman in Queensland in 1898 described how 'young lubras were taken to the station for licentious purposes, and there kept more like slaves than anything else. I have heard it said that these same lubras have been locked up for weeks at a time.' I pored over an old photograph for a long time, trying to interpret it: a naked young Aboriginal woman stood in long grass looking woebegone while beside her a settler stared cockily at the camera. Did the long grass hide rope or chains around her ankles?

A settler wrote a letter referring to the Aboriginal people as 'vermin' and urging his correspondent to 'Shoot them all and manure the ground with them!'

The murder of Aboriginal people was a crime for which white men could be hanged, and occasionally they were. That discouraged the reporting of killings. But at least two large-scale killings left an excellent paper trail because the perpetrators were brought to trial, and several of them were executed.

At Waterloo Creek in northern New South Wales in 1838 (the year Wiseman died), a large group of Aboriginal people was ambushed as they camped by a waterhole and an unknown number (accounts varied between four and 300) were killed. At Myall Creek, not far away, the Aboriginal men were sent off working and their women and children, with a few older men, were tied together, force-marched to a clearing and hacked to death. The bodies were burned: the fire was tended for a full day but a witness some time later could still see the half-burned remains of between twenty and thirty people.

Taking notes about these atrocities made me feel sick. I could feel my eyes going starey and fixed, close to tears. My pen moved slowly over the page. The last time I'd felt like this—shocked, tainted—was when, as a student, I'd accidentally come across a book full of pictures of people in the Nazi death camps.

The poisoned, dirtied feeling came from the closeness of these events. They hadn't happened on the other side of the world. The Waterloo Creek and Myall Creek massacres occurred within a hundred kilometres of my mother's birthplace. They weren't done by the Ku Klux Klanners or Afrikaners I'd been brought up to despise for their racism.

These were my own people.

The perpetrators were separated from me by time and culture, that was true. Solomon Wiseman and his neighbours grew up in a crueller world than my own. And there was the logic of the situation, too, of newcomers moving into a place where other people were already living. One set of people wanted things another set already had. How could there *not* be trouble?

Reminding myself of that wasn't enough to make the sick feeling go away.

But the historians drew a complex, nuanced picture of those times. Among the stories of brutality were others of honourable, even courageous behaviour by settlers. At great cost to himself, the ex-convict David Carly in Western Australia in the late nineteenth century protested to the authorities about the mistreatment of Aboriginal people:

> Again I write to you...from this land of murder and slavery and fraud...I have defended these murdered Slaves to the best of my ability for 13 years and to my Complete Ruin so I will defend them to the last as I have long since given up all hope of aid from any quarter.

In South Australia in 1838 the settler Robert Cock, a Quaker, insisted on paying 'rent' to the Aboriginal people for the land he occupied. Other settlers wrote of their friendships with Aboriginal people. I read several accounts of white men who lived with their Aboriginal wives and children and protected them, in spite of the hostility of their own society.

All of these people, black and white, had been faced with choices about what to do in situations they'd never encountered before. They'd made their choices under the influence of all sorts of factors: self-interest, morality, peer pressure, fear. They had made both good and terrible decisions. What choices had my great-great-great grandfather made?

What choices would I have made?

16
Aboriginal Voices

Aboriginal people were quoted in the history books I was reading, but not very often. Even when they spoke English, the first Australians in those early days generally didn't read or write it well enough to create a record. So finding out, for example, what might have been in the old man's mind when Phillip gave him those three slight slaps was never going to be easy.

I ploughed through a couple of books by white anthropologists. They seemed obsessed with marriage rules—I read an awful lot about moieties and kin groups. It was like reading about insects or molecules: distant, unhuman. It was a long way from *what was it really like?*

But one book led to another, from specialised academic

volumes to small-press local histories. I was starting to realise how wrong my preconceptions about Aboriginal life and culture were. That word 'nomad', for instance. Traditional Aboriginal people moved around, true, but within a precisely defined territory. Everyone knew exactly where the boundaries were. If strangers came onto your territory without asking permission, you were entitled to make them leave.

This wasn't quite what I'd have called a 'nomad'. It sounded more like the way I moved at home from the bedroom to the living room and out into the garden. I walked around, but I knew exactly where my place ended and the next-door place began, and so did everyone else.

Then there was the business of being a 'hunter and gatherer'. Now I was learning about complicated stone fish-traps built on rivers to ensure a permanent supply of fish; about the way fruit seeds were spat into middens of shells and bones so that more trees would grow there; about breeding pairs of possums being carried to places where they were scarce. I read about how regular, systematic burning of the bush created pasture land for game.

This wasn't quite my picture of 'hunting and gathering'. In fact, some of it sounded very like farming.

Aboriginal culture was hard to get a clear look at. It took me a long time to work out that that was the point. In my culture, knowledge was public. Even sacred stuff was open to everyone. If you wanted to know what the Bible was about, you went along to a Bible class.

In the Aboriginal way of doing things, it seemed to be different. This was a culture in which knowledge was sacred, and sacred often meant secret. Certain people—and only certain people—had the right to certain kinds of knowledge.

The stories that carried the knowledge had many levels. The elementary levels could be told to children (and white people), but there were deeper layers of meaning that few were allowed to know.

I gathered, too, that stories operated somewhat in the manner of title deeds. If you'd been told the story—the full story, not the public version—about a particular piece of country, it was part of what gave you the right to be on it.

But you didn't *own* it. You could use it, you were responsible for it. You were its custodian. But as an individual you didn't own land.

In fact, you didn't really own anything. Food, for instance. The group got the food, and then divided it out among everyone. There seemed to be no idea of competing with each other to get more food, or more land, or a better house—the things that people competed over in my culture. Even art—the ultimate expression of the individual in my world—wasn't the expression of an individual sensibility.

This was what Mum would call 'an eye-opener'. No matter how much I read, I still couldn't really get my head around it all. It was so foreign.

It took a long time to realise that that was an appropriate feeling. I *was* an outsider to this culture. This wasn't knowledge you could expect to go to a book and learn. The thing was to recognise that I didn't know.

I could see, though, how blindly I'd been embedded in my own culture. I'd never recognised it as a culture—a learned thing. I thought it was part of being human to compete for things of value. Now I saw that it was part of *my group's* way of being human. In my culture, the way for the species to survive was through competition. In Aboriginal culture, on a different part of the planet, the best way to survive was through sharing and collaborating.

It started to make sense of what happened between white and black two hundred years ago. Not only did both have different systems of belief about how people should behave—they often didn't realise that they were operating within a system of belief. Each group thought its behaviour was normal. Neither could see any kind of sense in the way the other was behaving.

The land looked empty and unclaimed to the newcomers because it had none of the familiar marks of ownership: fences, roads, houses. It was perhaps understandable that they thought they were entitled to take it up.

But from the Aboriginal point of view it must have seemed that strangers had come in and annexed the back verandah, or the kitchen, put a fence around it and defended it with guns.

You could get by without your verandah, but you might starve if the kitchen was taken, and that's what those fertile river flats on the Hawkesbury were. When the strangers grew corn, and grazed sheep, it must have seemed reasonable to pick the corn, spear the sheep.

No wonder there'd been trouble.

I understood a lot more now, and I was glad I'd waited before speaking to Aboriginal people. If I was anxious about what kind of settler Wiseman had been, that was my own issue. I had to deal with it myself. I couldn't ask Aboriginal people to help me with it.

But I also felt the importance of speaking, if I could, to descendants of the Aboriginal people Wiseman would have met. The story about my ancestor intersected with their stories. Talking to them wasn't research, it was a matter of courtesy.

One of the things I'd learned in the course of my reading was that it was as useful to talk about 'the Aboriginal people' as it was to talk about 'the European people'.

Where Wiseman settled was the country of the Darug. The other side of the Hawkesbury was Darkinjung country. They were different groups, with different (though related) languages.

The Darug was one of the groups which bore the full brunt of European expansion. The smallpox epidemic in 1789 killed many of them. Many of the attacks the *Gazette* described were made by Darug men and many of those killed would have been Darug. Those first thirty years of warfare, disease and displacement must have severely disrupted their culture.

This meant that the Darug weren't easy to learn much about, two hundred years later. But there were descendants who were reconstructing the language and the culture. I asked around, found a contact and picked up the phone.

I expected a polite rebuff, but Auntie Edna Watson, a Darug elder, and later another descendant, John Gallard, heard me out while I tried to explain. Solomon Wiseman my ancestor. My need to fill in some of the holes in the family story. My awareness that the story I was exploring wasn't a comfortable one.

Trying to explain made me realise how little I knew what I was doing and where all this obsessive work might lead me.

As these Darug people began to speak to me I listened and scribbled, page after page. They told me some stories I knew already, others I didn't: stories about boys thrown into the river to die, about men's hands being cut off, about burnings and shootings.

And they told me about the yam daisies.

Yam daisies are edible tubers that used to grow in vast numbers on the river-flats. They have a yellow flower a bit like a dandelion and a cluster of tubers that—in John's words—'hung down like the fingers of a hand'. The Darug dug them up and ate the roots, but would re-plant one of the 'fingers' so there'd be a crop again the following year.

Listening to them tell me about those yam daisies, I began to realise how important they were. They were a staple of the Darug diet, the source of bulk and carbohydrate, playing the same role that potatoes did in the Irish diet. Fish and game and other plants were added to that staple but wouldn't always have been enough on their own.

The yam daisies grew on the same rich soil that the Europeans chose for their own crops. The newcomers dug them up as weeds, and planted corn and wheat. When the Darug people came back, expecting to harvest their yam daisies, and found them replaced by other crops, they harvested them instead.

After I got off the phone I sat for a long time looking out at the front yard, trying to absorb the significance of what I'd learned.

The story of the yam daisies made sense of conflict all over the country. It was the story of settlement in miniature. One event came after another, no one understood what the other side was thinking, and at the end there was bad trouble. It was never a simple matter of right and wrong.

Thinking back to that scene with Governor Phillip and the man he'd slapped, I still didn't understand it. But I could see now that there were whole grammars of behaviour, dictionaries of culture, that would make sense of the 'old man's' actions. Things to do with the protocols of being a guest and a host, with giving and taking, with respect and authority.

I was appalled at the misunderstanding that must have

happened in that moment, even though all parties had only good will towards each other. How easy it was for things to go wrong. Once they'd gone wrong, how hard to put right.

I'd lived in one kind of Australia all my life. Now I was glimpsing a different country I'd been living in too, but never seen. I'd been to Wiseman's place. Now I had to go back again, but this time to the Aboriginal place.

17

The Bush at Night

The road was familiar now. The two-car garages, the three-car garages, the retirement villages. The bags of manure.

Around the last hairpin bends, past the pub, down to the ferry. Drive on diagonally. The river, the cliffs, a breeze along the water making dark cats-paws.

I was crossing the boundary between Darug and Darkinjung land as I crossed the river. Wiseman's was on Darug land. Where I was going—the campground—was on Darkinjung land. I was glad I knew that now. It made me look at the river and see it doubled: the river I'd seen before, plus this new one.

Darug and Darkinjung would have visited each other. Bark canoes. I'd read about those. And they probably swam across too. The current looked strong today, the tide pouring downstream. But if you picked the right time it would be an easy enough swim.

Off the ferry, it was turn right along the road that hugged the base of the cliff. There'd probably always been a track here, so the Darkinjung could get along the river. I was looking out for the road that branched off up the escarpment. The Darkinjung, too, would have wanted to get up onto the plateau where I was going. The white man's double-grooved track probably followed the course of an ancient path.

Feeling the nose of the car tilt up the steep dirt track, I felt a moment's apprehension. Not long before, some hikers had nearly died up here, confused by the deep gullies and sharp ridges of this dry stony wilderness. They'd been found, but only in the nick of time.

I made sure that the water bottle was where I packed it, and still full. I wished I'd remembered to check the pressure in my spare tyre. The mobile was no use to me here: the peaks all around cut off the signal. I was on my own. Even Wiseman stayed behind at the ferry.

The first part of the drive seemed almost vertical, the road screwing its way up. At the top it flattened, the landscape opened out. The vegetation was thinner and pricklier, the air astringent, almost medicinal.

From this high point I could see miles in every direction, and everywhere it was nothing but ridges and gullies, ridges and gullies, each one woolly with bush, bluer and bluer into the distance.

I stopped the car and got out. The waiting silence swallowed the sound of the engine. A crow mocked me from somewhere: *caar, caaar, caaaaar*. The sky was a pale empty blue.

Wilderness. This was what wilderness was.

I could see an outcrop of rock that promised an even greater vista, but I had to force myself to leave the road. Only twenty metres, I told myself. What are you scared of? It was hard going. At every step I had to push a bush aside, or loop around a fallen tree, or detour to avoid a thicket of saplings. At times an opening looked like a path and tempted me to follow it, but it always ended in another thicket.

I was panting, although I'd walked such a short way: not so much from exertion as a sort of tightness in my chest that you could have called anxiety. Around me the bush was full of noise: an underlying hum and tick, the drone of a million insects; closer individual clicks and twitters; the birds going *eep eep eep*.

It was all bursting with life, but also utterly empty. I glanced back. The bushes seemed to have closed behind me, smoothly, silently, like water. Which way was the road? In making those loops and detours, which way had I gone? All around me, the shadows twitched, light and dark shifting together among trunks, bushes, rocks.

For an instant I let the idea of *lost* into my mind. It would be so easy to flounder on, through the formless up and down of it, the land bafflingly twisting back on itself, each ridge and gully looking like the next. In these miles of indifferent ridges, the thin wavering line of the road was the only thing made by people, and even that was invisible until you stumbled out of the bush and found yourself standing on it.

I looked down at my shoes, something familiar. I reminded myself of the idea of *behind* and *in front*. The road was behind me. If I turned, it would be there.

Back on the track I realised I'd been holding my breath.

Silly. A few steps into the bush and I'd panicked. It seemed important to remind myself that my panic wasn't a moral shortcoming, but an interesting thing to know. Wiseman didn't have that track. Not *behind*, not *in front*. He had a whole continent stretching away around him, and those birds that made the place sound so very empty.

After the miles of dry ridges, the campground in the hollow was an oasis: a big clear area with soft bright grass, scattered trees, sunlight glancing between the trunks. A swift creek caught the light as it ran over plates of rock.

The silence was broken only by the occasional smack of whip-birds and the warbling of magpies. It was easy to imagine that nothing had changed here for two hundred years, even two thousand. Just the creek and the grass, and the breeze in the branches above me. I felt like the first human in the first, perfect garden.

I took off my shoes to walk along the creek. The water on my skin was cold and clean. Under my feet I could feel bumps in the rocks, shallow grooves the length of a hand. When I squatted down and looked sideways I could see that they were the colour of the rest of the rock but not part of its natural form. There were dozens, hundreds, all over the flat rocks.

It was a jolt, as if someone had shoved me hard in the back, to realise what they were. These weren't some strange act of nature. They were made by humans. They were grinding grooves, where people put an edge on their stone axes. I'd seen the pictures in books.

This entire creek was a whetstone.

In an instant wilderness transformed itself under my feet into workshop. Generation after generation of people had ground their axes here. In this sweet glade they had eaten, slept, made love, had babies.

Forget feeling like the first human.

And forget any cosy illusions about Wiseman. This country wouldn't have seemed like wilderness when he was here. He couldn't have pretended for a moment that it was an empty land. Along every stream, the thousands of axe-grinding grooves would have been clear and fresh, the newly scraped stone gold against the dark. Narrow sandy paths would have wound through the trees. The trees themselves would have carried fresh bleeding wounds where canoes and shields had been prised out of the bark. Every rock overhang would have been blackened by a cooking fire, scattered with bones and shells from past meals. Wiseman would have known that every acre of this place was as lived in as his own house.

No wonder he thought he had to build a fortress.

The campfire later was a comfort, a room made of light, carved out of the darkness, with myself safe at the centre.

But it blinded too. You had a choice. You could feel safe, but be blind. Or you could see, and know how small you were.

I'd lit the fire, cooked my meal, heaped the wood on to push the darkness back. Now I let the flames die, the embers darken. It was time to see what was out there.

The bush at night was like a great sighing lung. Up on the ridge that encircled the hollow, a wind was blowing, but down here only the occasional shaft of breeze came through.

In the pauses between breaths, the night noises. A flurry and rustle, a small thump. Certain private sounds—*pwik pwik pwik*. Close at hand, the breeze was smaller, more personal, the flutter of one bunch of leaves at a time, a shaft of cooler air like the draught from an open door. With the fire burned away to nothing, the trees were bigger and closer. They leaned down, soft shaggy creatures, watching.

I was restless, alert. Almost as if I was waiting for something. Not that I was frightened, exactly. Nothing here was malevolent, nothing was hostile. This place wasn't going to spook me.

But there wasn't *nothing*, either. This was an empty place—but empty the way a room was when the people had that minute walked out of it. They left a blank, but the blank held the shape of their presence. I wasn't feeling the emptiness of the place, but the once-fullness of it.

The wind was swelling again through the trees up on the ridge, each individual leaf adding its voice to the choir of moving air. It filled out of the silence into a stately roar of sound that travelled around the hillside, held its breath, then faded, tree by tree, leaving only a long pause that waited and listened.

Listening, waiting for the next respiration of the wind, I realised how far I'd travelled in my search for Wiseman and his world. A year before, I'd known almost nothing about him, and less about the place he'd come to and the people who'd been there before him. If I'd thought about telling a story, it had been a shallow one, blinkered by my ignorance: a biography at most, or perhaps an appendix to the family story, a few more details to be handed down to future generations.

Now, sitting so small in this immense airy night, I was beginning to sense the real dimensions of this thing. There was a story here that was bigger than my ancestor, bigger even than the tale of his relationship to the Aboriginal people. It was about the life that the place held within itself, within its rocks and trees. The place was speaking to me as I sat listening, and although I couldn't hear it properly, and didn't know how to tell its story, I knew I was going to try.

PART TWO

18

Starting to Write

At the end of 1968, after my final exams at school, I decided to write a novel. I spent many happy hours planning it and writing an outline for each chapter. Then I wrote Chapter One at the top of a fresh sheet of paper and started fleshing out the outline.

Writing the book wasn't nearly as much fun as doing the outline.

Pride and obstinacy got me labouring along as far as the end of Chapter Two, and then I looked at the outline for Chapter Three: 'Louise meets John at the beach—they're reading the same book—they exchange phone numbers—Louise wonders if she's in love—John doesn't ring.'

A weariness came over me at the thought of *fleshing this out.*

I closed the exercise book and put it away. I never wrote in it again.

A few years later I had another couple of goes at novels in the same tightly planned way. I even managed to write two of them. It was boring writing them and I knew it was boring reading them. In a half-hearted way I tried to find a publisher, but when no one wanted them I wasn't surprised.

Then one day in my late twenties I lay on the bed of the shared house I was living in. I was reading *The Letters of Jane Austen* (possibly to find out if she wrote from chapter outlines) and listening to Mr Next-Door's dog yapping through its hopeless afternoon. I came across the sentence, 'In the night we invent a few hard names for the stars.' Who knew what Jane Austen meant by it, but it set off a vivid image in my mind: that famous bag-lady, Bea Miles, who'd offered recitations from Shakespeare on the steps of the Mitchell Library and was famous for having once taken a taxi thousands of miles to the Nullarbor to pick wildflowers. For a time she'd lived in a stormwater drain in Rushcutter's Bay Park. I imagined her in her drain, looking up at the stars and inventing hard names for them.

Without having any idea of where I was going, I wrote five or six pages by free association, using Austen's words as a trigger. Reading them back, I realised I wanted to know more about Bea Miles. I knew the bare outline of her life, enough to have a question—what had happened to get her to the steps of the Mitchell Library offering recitations from Shakespeare? I realised that to write out of a question was as good as—perhaps better than—writing out of an answer.

To imagine a story for Bea Miles, I didn't research and I didn't do a chapter outline. I started work each day by glancing through some 'interesting things'—more of those Jane Austen letters, bits of Shakespeare, the letters of Flaubert, old-fashioned household hints about how to keep the moths out of fur coats, photographs of schoolgirls from 1912 in big lace collars. I'd allow the bits to suggest something that might have happened to my bag-lady character—an event that involved putting furs away for the summer, a memory of herself in a big lace collar—and write without a plan, following thoughts and images into the unknown, until I ran out of steam. Then I'd plunge back into the 'interesting bits' until something else got me going.

The criterion was energy. If I felt energised in writing a fragment or a scene, I'd keep going. If it began to feel like a chore, I ruled a line under it in the exercise book and started again.

It had worked. I called the novel *Lilian's Story*. It was satisfying to write, got published, and even won a prize.

From that experience I'd developed a few mantras about writing. *Never have a blank page* was one. *Don't wait for the mood*: that was another, because you could always *fix it up later*.

In the years after *Lilian's Story* was published, our children Tom and Alice were born, and I added another mantra: *Don't wait for time to write*. I learned to work in whatever slivers of time the day might give me—one of my favourite scenes in *Joan Makes History* was written in the car waiting to pick up Tom from a birthday party, on the only paper I could find, the inside of a flattened Panadol packet. I had slivers of time, so I wrote in slivers of words: a page here, a paragraph there. Eventually the slivers would add up to something.

I wrote four more novels using that makeshift method. But I didn't think it would work for *The Wiseman Book*, as I thought of this project, because it wouldn't be a novel.

I wanted to tell the story of what I'd learned about the frontier, to explore that sad history of fear, misunderstanding and violence. It was a tale that drew its power from the fact that it was real. Interposing a layer of invention would defeat my aim: to tell the unvarnished story as truthfully as I could.

My workroom was the front room at home. It had too many things in it: two desks, two filing cabinets, two bookcases. A couch. A cello (in fact, until Alice grew that extra few inches, two cellos: a big one for me and a smaller one for her), music stool, music stand. Piles of books. The big sideboard thing that had been Grandma's.

The window above my desk looked out onto the front yard, a constantly changing landscape of building materials and other objects brought home by Tom: a massive beam of wood, a stack of six brown shutters, several sheets of scavenged plywood, an antique pram with the word SWAN in curly letters along the side, a person-sized roll of silver bubble wrap and a prop from a university production of *Snow White*, a throne that doubled as a coffin.

Not long after that night in the bush on Darkinjung land I sat down with a brand new spiral bound exercise book and my favourite kind of rollerball pen.

I tried not to ask myself, *what are you planning to do, exactly?* because I didn't know. *Never have a blank page*, I reminded myself, and started talking onto the page, thinking aloud:

'Form—like <u>The First Stone</u> or <u>Stravinsky's Lunch</u>—non-fiction, but a conversational style. Vignettes. Chapters like Moby Dick—for example a chapter called <u>On Doing Family History</u>. Some elements of memoir.'

Some elements of memoir. Who was I kidding with this pompous tone?

But seeing this made me realise that I was already looking for a shape for the book. The fact that there were precedents—Drusilla Modjeska's book about women artists, Helen Garner's about a case of sexual harassment—was reassuring. I didn't have to reinvent the wheel.

Suddenly I was all fired up. I stared past the front yard, past our crookedly clipped hedge, over the top of the house across the road, into the sky, empty except for a television aerial.

I could see this book, feel it, almost taste it as I stared up at that odd-shaped patch of blue framed by the neighbour's roof and the edge of our upstairs porch. It would be a wonderful and subtle mix of memoir, history and speculation. I'd allow myself flights of fancy—elements of fiction, you might say—where I put flesh on the bones of what I'd found out. Modjeska and Garner had both done that, and it gave their books richness and life without compromising their factual basis.

I got the pen moving across the paper again: 'Never had faith in a book before and never had this <u>urge, craving</u> to get to it. Always an effort before. Now—real excitement plus sense of doing something <u>worth doing</u>.'

And I didn't have to start where I usually did: with the nothing out of which a novel must be drawn like a spider's thread. I had all these notes.

They were heaped up in one of the bookcases: four high piles of bulging manila folders with titles scrawled on the spines. 'London—Wiseman's places.' 'Research—books—Aboriginal people.' 'Family history.'

There were forty-seven folders. The folders had labels, but they didn't really tell you what was inside. I'd found that my idea about tidy card catalogues and colour-coded this, that and the other didn't work when applied to the real world. Should information about the Old Bailey go in the folder called 'London—Wiseman's Places', for example, or the one called 'Convicts'?

Inside each folder was a muddle of scrawled notes, photocopied pages, pictures torn out of magazines, newspaper clippings. I opened a few. Each bit of paper was interesting, but nothing went with anything else.

Just keep writing, I told myself:

Need to make a list of where to go next. Can't see how to organise what I've already got. Already a muddle. Overlap, the researcher's problem—life isn't in tidy boxes. My feeling of smug control, tidying history away into compartments starting to evaporate. Still the desire to control, limit, categorise. My feeling that the sad muddle of the past can be reduced to a succession of neat questions with or without answers—that I can stay outside it all, in charge. But it's already a muddle.

Two birds landed on the TV aerial across the road—a big one and a very small one. They perched there facing the same way like two people on a bus.

I was slowing down. My rule of thumb was to cover at least five pages a day with writing. It didn't have to be good writing or even useable writing. It just had to cover the pages. So I kept going.

In the same way that I'd skimmed through *The Letters of Jane*

Austen all those years ago, I skimmed through the transcript of the Old Bailey trial. The drama of the moment leapt out at me again, as freshly as when I first read it, and got me writing:

> For God's sake Mr Rowey have mercy, you know the consequence. What was in his mind as he pinched those lumps of Brazil timber was that if he was caught he'd be killed by having a hard rope put around his neck and he'd be suspended from it, perhaps killed outright but more likely die a slow & excruciating death by suffocation, his hands tied behind his back, his feet kicking frantically at air, with a crowd watching, perhaps you'd hear them laughing and calling out as you flailed and twirled (find eye-witness account of a hanging) in a blind congested panic of airlessness.
>
> Find out about the physiological realities of hanging & how they would have done it at Newgate in 1805.
>
> Would Sol have seen a public hanging? When did it stop being public?
>
> No man shall know the hour of his death & just as well. The whole of the time leading up to it would be spent in horror & grief & panic. Watching each minute, each second tick away. This is my second-last sunset, the last time I go to the toilet, the last time I will ever blow my nose. Apart from the physical pain & fright of execution the worst part of the punishment would be knowing for sure, exactly, to the minute, how long you had left. We all know death is a finite number of nose-blows away, but that knowledge isn't really something we can live with.

Over the next six months, I wrote many pages like this, about Newgate, about Wiseman's early life in London, about what it might have been like to be a lighterman on the Thames.

Then I started opening the other set of manila folders, the ones about Australia. I wrote about what things were like in Sydney in 1806, about the convict system, about the way convicts were assigned to free settlers as servants, about the 'ticket of leave' system. Now and then I'd write something that could be called 'some elements of memoir':

Wiseman would certainly have had reason to go to Government House at Parramatta, perhaps to receive his pardon.

The thing that strikes you about it today is how small it is, how humble it seems. It's a plain square box of a building softened only by a graceful roofline, shutters along the windows, and a columned entranceway.

In front of Government House in 1806, the gently sloping ground down to the Parramatta River was the site of a convict camp. It's grass now, with the odd gum tree. There's a sign that tells me that if I look to my left I can see the 'shadow' of the road that serviced that convict encampment. *Oh, come off it, what's this shadow business,* I think, but I glance to my left—and there, like a photograph rising up out of the blank paper in the developing dish, is indeed the shadow of a road, a different texture in the grass, a scar in the ground that's still visible after nearly two hundred years.

I had some lunch down there near the river. There's a man down there in the dirt-coloured suit of a derro, his face and hands dark with dirt. He gets in and out of a car so ancient and rusty, so planted to the spot that I realise it's not so much a car as a dwelling-place. He's watching me as if he's waiting for me to go so he can get on with his life. I've invaded his front yard.

By July 2001, I had about a hundred pages of writing. Some bits were lively, but lots of it was dry and dead. Never mind. I could fix it up later.

19
The Assembly

Before I was a writer, I'd been a film editor. Not a very good one, and not for long. But a few films included my name on the credits.

I'd worked on some *cinema verité* documentaries. The director started out with only a rough sketch of a script. The idea was to go out and shoot life, as it happened. Later, in the editing room, you'd find the story in the shots. That's what I had to do now: go through what I had written and find a structure for all those fragments.

Outside my workroom window the shutters and the roll of silver bubble wrap had been replaced by three glass-paned doors, a lawn-mower with a broken handle, and a clothes dryer that was perfectly good except that the door didn't shut.

The pram was still there, but it was full of mirror tiles now. At my desk I was making lists.

What I've got:

1. The Family Story
2. Sol's London
3. Lighterman
4. Sydney in 1805
5. Crime & punishment
6. Sol on Hawkesbury
7. Aboriginal people on Hawkesbury
8. Sol after 1826
9. Descriptions of Sol—the portraits.

I named a new document on the computer, *Assembly draft 1*, and arranged my bits of writing according to the list. Something was not right. I tried another kind of list:

Preliminary outline—Sol's Story.

1. Which Wiseman was he?
2. Crime & punishment
3. Arrival in Sydney
4. A free man again
5. Bankrupt
6. Land grant
7. The man of property
8. Wife dead.

Another new document, *Assembly draft 2*, another few weeks of rearranging. As I went, I subdivided some of the pieces, deleted some, rewrote others, and wrote new ones.

Then yet another list called 'Preliminary outline' and another new document. *Assembly draft 3*, *Assembly draft 4*, *Assembly draft 5*, *Assembly draft 6*.

All the lists looked great. But as soon as I tried to make the writing correspond, everything went wrong.

Most of it was boring, that was one problem. Pages and pages of stuff about the assignment system and how important yam daisies were. The order worried me, too. Should I begin in 1788 with Governor Phillip slapping that old man? Or with Wiseman in London?

And there was something about the tone I didn't like. The 'memoir' bits had a jocular feel, like a clergyman visiting a kindergarten. The 'research' bits were terrible—where did that awful starchy schoolmarm tone come from? Surely not me?

The main problem, though, was something I was reluctant to face. I was determined to write a book of non-fiction, but the only parts of this 'assembly' that were interesting were the 'flights of fancy' where I'd created the flesh to put on the bones of research. Where, in a word, I'd written fiction.

The mirror tiles had gone from the pram and the dryer was replaced by two non-working whipper-snippers. What was wrong with this book wasn't the order of the pieces. It was the writing itself. I could either write a truthful book that would be so dull as to be unreadable, or I could write a made-up book that might be read but not believed.

It had all seemed so wonderfully simple that night in the bush, listening to the wind.

20

The Fictional Quester

When I was a short-sighted child, reading was my whole life. I read in the bath, I read on the toilet, I read under the desk at school, I read up in my treehouse, feeling the branches of the jacaranda swell and subside under me.

One of the unforeseen griefs of becoming a writer was that I could no longer lose myself in a book the way I had as a child. I still read, of course, but now part of me was always watching how the writer had done it. There was always something to learn, something I could try in my own writing. It was a rare and compelling book that made me forget that it had been *made*.

One morning in October 2001 I lay on the couch in my workroom, delaying the journey to the desk, where I was starting to hate my latest assembly draft. I promised myself I could read for half an hour. It was warmer under the rug on the couch, too. In spite of a new gas heater, my workroom was draughty and a cold spring wind was pouring in around the window frame.

Anil's Ghost, by Michael Ondaatje, is a very good book, but that wasn't why I stayed there reading it for the rest of the morning. I was wolfing it down because Michael Ondaatje was telling me what to do.

Anil's Ghost is a novel. Its main character is invented. But it is based on historical events, and some of the characters are apparently versions of real people. Ondaatje's main character is on a quest to uncover a hidden episode of history.

I was thinking that Ondaatje was showing me a way out of my deadlock. The 'I' character in *The Wiseman Book*, the 'quester', was myself—but it didn't have to be. I could try the sleight of hand that Ondaatje had pulled off: to fictionalise the quester, but not the quest. I could step out of the limelight, leaving the search for Wiseman and his dealings with Aboriginal people centre stage.

Sitting at the desk with the rug now wrapped around my legs against the fierce draught under the door, I thought about my fictional quester. He or she would be around my own age. He or she might have had a country childhood—even better, have grown up on the Hawkesbury. He or she would come across some evidence of a massacre—half-burned bones, something like that. He or she would start to think about those bones and what they meant. He or she would go off on a quest to find out the story behind them. And so on.

Thank you, Michael Ondaatje.

I glanced through the folder called 'London—Wiseman's

Places' and saw a note I'd made watching the tide turn on the Thames. No more lists, no more 'Preliminary Outlines'. Back to what I knew: free association. Not a novel, exactly, but using some of the novel's techniques. And, for me, the relief of being back on familiar territory.

> Across the surface of the river—pocked, pitted, rough—ran another kind of roughness, a buckle across the river from one side to the other, a ridge of water, and behind it, water of a different personality: barred, furrowed, a water more like the sea. Change of tide. The line moved imperceptibly upstream, making its way against the hidden force of the current, the river current meeting the tide current, colliding, creating this impasse, this ridge along the surface. Against the face of the ridge small waves broke as if against a wall, flicking and curling all the way along its length, tongues of water trying to mount the incoming pressure of water, but pushed back, back, pushing back into their own pressure, the tide moving in its slow line up past Horselydown Old Stairs, past Suffrance Dock, up past Tower Stairs.

I stopped there. I'd run out of things to say about the change of tide on the Thames. But I skimmed another few pages in the folder and came across something Melissa Lucashenko had said in London about how illiterate people read the world in ways other than through words, and it sparked off a connected idea about Wiseman:

> He'd been ashamed, in the grand church, with the columns that vanished high up into shadows, the ceiling out of sight, like God himself—been ashamed of his big fist grasping

the feather, the cracked fingertips clumsy, like pieces of wood, as he scratched the nib down and then across where the curate's white finger pointed, a blank space hemmed around with delicate spidery marks hardly the same species as his own thick lines, with a spot and a spatter where the nib had been crushed too hard against the paper. Solomon Wiseman, the curate had said, pointing. His mark. There, if you please.

He had got ink on his finger, that thick wooden finger. Later, at the Cauliflower, lifting the tankard, he'd seen it and been ashamed all over again, this mockery of an ink-stain, in the same spot on the first finger that the curate himself had had an ink-stain, as if he were pretending to be some other kind of man.

I enjoyed writing the London scenes. I felt I could go on writing them forever. I had the bed of detail from all that research, so I could see in my mind's eye what I was writing about. It was real. I'd been there, I'd seen it. I even had objects: that bit of roof tile, now on my desk, a big map of early London on the wall. From the real, it was a leap to inventing a world and Wiseman in it, but at least I had something to trigger off those free associations.

Halfway through the second exercise book I glanced at what I'd been doing. It was all London, and I hadn't even started to cover all that could be written about London.

I wrote a stern note to myself:

To Do:

1. Sketch the rest of the London scenes
2. Assemble London chronologically

3. MOVE ON TO AUSTRALIA!!!!

Only near the end of that second handwritten book was there anything set in Australia, a scene in which Wiseman was looking at the Hawkesbury and comparing it to London:

> Looking down at the brown river, where he could see the water seething and dimpling with the flood tide, he said, think of it as the Thames before civilization, my dear. Here we are standing in Bermondsey with our feet sinking in the mire and the water pouring in—Butler's Buildings could go right here and not feel out of place!
>
> Jane stared out glumly. He saw her trying to force a smile, but the corners of her mouth still turned down.
>
> It is the same width as the Thames, look pet, and brown like our own river, the tide comes in and out the same way; this is the Thames, as it was seen by our ancestors, before even the Romans.

Like me, Wiseman was putting off making the move to the southern hemisphere.

The hard part of the writing wasn't finding the words—they seemed to come reasonably easily. If they started to come reluctantly, I stopped and began with something else. The hard part was finding the picture. Once I could see and hear the moment, I could write it. But there were long gaps between one burst of writing and another, times of frustration when I couldn't get the picture clear, or couldn't see anything at all. The worst times were when I tried to write the scene anyway, throwing words at something I couldn't see or hear.

The phrases would come more and more slowly, each sentence an effort. I'd read it back and groan aloud at the deadness of it. It was dead because it was phoney. I was just making it up out of words, so words were all I had: clichés, pedestrian images, abstractions. No pictures, no sounds, no smells—no life.

If I could get the picture in my mind—Wiseman looking up at the columns in Christ Church Spitalfields, the white marble steps under his feet—I could set it all in motion and see what would happen. Perhaps it's like improvising in the theatre: you have the situation, and you make up what might happen next. Sooner or later you get to a point where it all stops, and then you have to backtrack and start again, or jump sideways until an incident begins to unfold and the writing flows.

In my struggle to see and hear what I was writing, I used whatever came to hand. I overheard Alice and her friend Ellie on the back steps after school one day having a spitting competition. I didn't take notes or plan to use that—but the next day I found myself writing a scene in which Wiseman, as a child, had a spitting competition with his sweetheart Sophia. It made a nice warm moment between them.

I spent a couple of nights in the public ward of a hospital and made a note on a paper towel about one of the other women in the room: 'Old Mrs Priestley—her cough the only strong thing about her.' When I got home and found the paper towel in my handbag, I gave that cough to Wiseman's mother. Then I realised that the cough meant she had TB, and that she'd died when Wiseman was barely more than a child.

It helped to smell as well as to see and hear. In the early documents I'd kept coming across references to something called a 'slush lamp'. What was it made of? What did you burn in it? What sort of light did it give?

A good child of the modern age, I Googled 'slush lamp' and to my surprise found several sites that told me it was a small dish full of fat, with a wick that hung into the fat and over the edge.

That night I cooked lamb chops for the family dinner, catching the fat in the griller. This I poured into a little dish. Then I cast about for a wick. Cotton, not too thick. A narrow strip of rag might do. I draped this into the fat, lit a match— flint and steel would have to wait for another day—and stood back.

In the next thirty seconds I learned more about life in a bark hut on the Hawkesbury in 1817 than all the books in the world could have told me. The slush lamp produced vast amounts of dense black smoke, which smelled powerfully of burned fat.

The flame was tiny, hardly making a dent in the darkness. Watching the fat burn away I realised that those settlers had had a choice: a scrape of dripping on their dry bread, or light at night. They couldn't afford both.

I went back to the desk and rewrote all the scenes in the hut at night.

I enjoyed making the slush lamp and I went through the draft, looking for other things I could try out. I travelled in a small boat along the Hawkesbury, made and ate 'hominy' and 'pease', had a go at making fire from two sticks (I couldn't even get them warm) and did a thousand other small experiments.

I filled another big exercise book, and by then I'd sketched out most of the story: Wiseman grows up in London, is transported to Australia, settles on the Hawkesbury, and comes into conflict with the Aboriginal people.

For that last part, I couldn't draw on my great-great-great grandfather, since there'd been no information about that part of his life. I adapted from other sources, giving to Wiseman the meeting between Governor Phillip and the 'old man' in Broken Bay, for example. I adapted loosely, but kept the basic shape of the encounter, and especially the piercing detail of the 'three slight slaps'.

Governor Macquarie's Proclamation, in which permission was given for settlers to shoot Aborigines, went into the writing exactly as it appeared in the *Gazette*.

The horrible details that I'd read about, of Aboriginal hands and ears being cut off, I gave to a character I called Smasher, whose name also came straight out of the notes I'd taken from the historians' books. I wrote a scene in which Aboriginal people were poisoned, adapted from nineteenth-century accounts. On the basis of several descriptions in the *Gazette* and information about 'penetrating injuries' from my doctor friends, I wrote a scene in which a settler died an agonising death from a spear.

The historical account of the Waterloo Creek massacre gave me details and phrases to create an episode in which Aboriginal people are ambushed and killed. I could see the place (a particular spot on the Macdonald River) even though I found the events hard to imagine.

These scenes of violence were the most difficult I'd ever written. Even now I don't want to look at them too closely. They had to be written because the story needed to include this aspect of the frontier, but I had to steel myself to get them done.

I didn't want the book to end with defeat for the Aboriginal people. I had in mind a short scene at the end in which something about the land itself would demonstrate that the Aboriginal people hadn't been destroyed:

> There was a tree by the river that had grown over a rock, a big curving lip of tree-flesh, growing down and you could see the tree would eventually cover the entire rock like an octopus flowing over its prey.
>
> But the tree, by the nature of being a thing that lived, would die, and there, underneath, would be the rock, not destroyed at all, ready to show itself to the sun for another thousand years.

It was a heavy-handed image for the idea I wanted to get across, a parallel that was much too neat. Tree equals settlers; rock equals Aboriginal people. No amount of tinkering with the words was ever going to make it work.

Never mind, *fix it up later.*

This first draft had a definite voice: stately, serious, even pompous. It used informal phrases now and then but it never used contractions. I hoped I could make it less precious later.

Some parts came out in the first person, sometimes it was in third person, but it was always from Wiseman's point of view.

The first-person point of view seemed right. The book was about the choices of one individual. I didn't want the reader to see him from the outside in an abstract way. I wanted the reader to be right there with him.

But by the time I was onto my fourth exercise book, it was clear that first person wasn't going to work. That stately voice didn't belong to an illiterate Thames lighterman. If the book was to be in the first person, the voice would have to become much rougher, less literary, to be convincing.

Peter Carey had published *The True History of the Kelly Gang* not long before. He'd brought off a virtuoso act of ventriloquism of exactly the sort I'd have to do if I wanted to write the book in Wiseman's voice. Carey had done it so well I was sure I'd only look foolish in attempting something similar.

I was also starting to see that there were things I wanted the book to say that Wiseman couldn't say. He didn't understand even the small amount I did about Aboriginal culture, for one thing. I knew that the Darug would starve without the yam daisies, but Wiseman didn't know that.

Third person it had to be, then, but 'third person subjective'—from Wiseman's point of view, but only partly in his voice.

I put off transcribing the contents of the exercise books into the computer, keeping that as a kind of reward. It wasn't until about March 2002 that I gave myself that treat.

The title was already in the machine from the day I read Michael Ondaatje's novel: *The Book of the Fictional Quester*. Now I started to type.

Some time later, I had a fat folder of printout and I knew for sure what I'd been suspecting for a while. There were no 'elements of memoir' in here at all. The fictional quester had never so much as put in an appearance. In spite of all my certainty that this book shouldn't be a novel, I'd written just that.

I sat staring past the laptop, out the window. Someone walked by on the other side of the hedge. I couldn't see the person through the screen of leaves, only the movement they were making. I sat very still. I liked to look out, but I hated thinking that people out there might be able to see me.

I was feeling the relief of a kid who's been told the maths homework had been cancelled. You knew you really should come to grips with surds, but oh the joy that you didn't have to.

But what about all those terrific reasons why this book couldn't be a novel? I was still sure that this subject matter had to be handled in the authoritative voice of non-fiction. It felt as though I'd come a very long way around to arrive at a dead end.

I sat scrolling up and down, reading bits and pieces. I corrected a few typos. I changed the font from Times New Roman to Georgia and made it 14 point instead of 12. I made it do a first-line indent. I did a word count. I wrote it at the end of the document—58,459—and sat staring at the blinking cursor telling me I'd come to the end.

I had no idea what to do with it now. It was time to abandon ship. Leave the desk, leave the house. Leave the words behind and revisit the place behind them.

The Land Speaking

The publican who put me up in Room 9 at the Wiseman's Ferry Inn had been exasperated when I'd quizzed him about the ghost's repertoire on the piano.

'Look, love, I've only been here six months. You want to know about Wiseman, you'd be best off asking Patrick.'

'Patrick?'

'Local feller, been here donkey's years.'

I whipped out my notebook and pen. 'Got a number for him? Know where he lives?'

The publican frowned but before he could say anything the phone rang down in the bar, and like a man reprieved he shot away to answer it. Over his shoulder, halfway down the stairs, he called back, 'In the bar, any time after four o'clock on a school day.' He sketched a man-sized shape on the air. 'Barefoot, blue singlet, big beard. Can't miss him.'

Now I was winding down those familiar hairpin bends above Wiseman's Ferry. What else was there to learn? I didn't know. But I felt that Wiseman's Ferry hadn't finished with me yet.

I drove down to Laughtondale and looked at where the old mill had been. I took another photo of the headstone for Solomon and Jane Wiseman. I drove along the river as far as Spencer. Trees, cliffs, water. Water, trees, cliffs.

I took more notes, I stood by mistake on a nest of ants, I saw a long dark snake side-wind across the road. I stepped out under the branches in a patch of mangroves and got one of my shoes sucked off by the mud.

I wasn't conscious of planning it, but at four o'clock I was back at the pub.

There was Patrick. Barefoot, blue singlet, big beard.

He heard me out as I stumbled through my story. Wiseman my great-great-great grandfather. Trying to piece together what happened. Writing a book.

I could hear my voice go uncertain on the word 'book'. But Patrick didn't ask any hard questions, like 'what sort of book?'

'Yes, well,' he said, 'I can show you a few things if you like.'

It was getting late, but we drove in his battered four-wheel-drive, up the hill to Courthouse Cave, where in the family story Wiseman sat in judgment over his convicts (except that in the story it was Judgment Rock). To Wiseman's Well, a dank mosquito-filled hollow where you could still see the flagstones lining a small pond.

As we looked around I learned a few things about Patrick,

mainly that he was a man whose greatest pleasure was to be in the bush. He wasn't indigenous, but he had a deep respect for the place and the people whose place it had always been.

I was probably the thousandth person to ask, but he patiently answered my questions about being barefoot in the bush. 'Your foot doesn't get hard like leather,' he said. 'More like a cellist's fingers—hard but sensitive as well.' Winter or summer, he told me, he wore the blue singlet and the shorts. 'I never feel cold,' he said. 'Give it the chance, your body adjusts.'

He voiced my thought: 'It's how the Aboriginal people could live here, they understood all that.'

The sun was dropping below the high ridge behind Wiseman's. I had to get back to Sydney. But Patrick offered to take me up into the bush another time.

He hardly knew me, had only heard a few words about what I thought I might be doing. But, as I came to learn, Patrick was a generous man as well as a knowledgeable one. Over the next couple of weeks we met several times and looked at many things.

He showed me a tree growing by the side of the road with a cigar-shaped scar four metres long in its side. The scar was made when a canoe was levered out of the bark, a hundred or so years ago. The scar started a couple of metres up the trunk. How did they get up that high? How did they lever out such a huge piece of bark in one piece without it splitting?

The tree was astonishing, but even more astonishing was that on my earlier visits, driving around looking for graveyards and so on, I'd sailed past it many times. I'd never noticed the scar. I might have looked, but I hadn't seen.

He showed me caves with stencils of hands: big hands, small hands, hand after hand outlined in white pipeclay on the rock. I held my own up beside one. A bit different around the thumb. But a hand like my own, greeting me.

He took me along the Macdonald Valley, knocked on the door of a house and asked permission to go into the backyard, down beside the river. There, under some plastic garden chairs and a skewiff plastic table, was an engraving in the rock: of a European ship, complete with mast, sails, rudder.

The owner of the garden setting got out the hose and squirted the engraving so we could see it more clearly. He and Patrick stood on the grass discussing whether it was an Aboriginal engraving or a whitefeller one.

I was thinking, *this could be Wiseman's own boat.*

Later, as the afternoon began to wear away, Patrick took me up along rough fire-trails, up and up through the National Park. We lurched along in his car, being lashed by branches, tossed about on the seats, onto the high ridges that I'd seen from the track to the campground.

When he turned off the engine the breathing of the bush came flowing into the silence, the sounds of it going about its life as it had always had. I followed Patrick along no track I could see, but he walked confidently into the mass of bushes and trees, glancing back occasionally to orient himself. Then he stopped. We were on a great open place among the trees where a flat platform of stone faced up at the sky. The place itself had such power—of space, of light, of some kind of intensity—that it took me a moment to see what was under our feet. Engravings, one after the other, grooved into the sandstone: kangaroos, emus, fish, humans. Not lined up neatly, but all over the surface of the rock, using its swells and dips to give the images life, each one at a different angle so you had to walk among them to see them and be drawn into the world they came from.

'What do they mean?' I asked.

'No one really knows,' he said. 'No one's left who knows the old stories.'

The engravings lay there on the surface of the rock, speaking up at the air. But there was no one who could hear them any more. There never would be again. Something was lost: not an extinct frog or flower, but an expression of the human spirit, the richness of its meaning vanished.

We stood on the rock platform as if silenced by the power of the place. Around us the leaves moved with a dry whispering sound. A big black bird perched on a branch and watched us with its yellow eye. Far up, in the pale sky, a cloud slowly shredded away to nothing.

I thought of the book that I was circling around, that I'd been trying so hard to control. It was the problem with having written a few books. You got cocky, thought you were the boss. You thought it was your book, to squeeze into this shape or that. Non-fiction. Memoir. The fictional quester.

How puny and little-minded all those plans seemed from the perspective of this ridge-top, in this vast room made of leaves and air. How presumptuous I'd been, thinking that this was my story alone, to pummel into shape as I saw fit, a story I understood enough to force into the form I wanted.

The breeze had picked up. The bunches of leaves whipped

against each other, whipped at the air. The place was speaking. It was a language I didn't know, but even so I was starting to understand.

How could I know what kind of book this was going to be? My job wasn't to take what I'd learned and squeeze it into the shape I thought it should have. Before it could be a book this was a story. That story was somehow part of all this—these trees, these rocks full of language that was lost. I didn't own that story. It had to be allowed to speak for itself. My job was to get out of its way.

PART THREE

22

What Have I Got?

A friend gave me a clip-on-a-stand that you could use to display a postcard. Into it I slipped the photo I'd taken of the tree with the canoe-shaped scar in its bark. It sat next to the piece of roof tile from the Thames.

I'd come back from Wiseman's Ferry after that day with Patrick full of a kind of calm energy. I knew what to do now, which was, in a manner of speaking, to do nothing.

First, do no harm. Wasn't that what doctors promised when they took the Hippocratic Oath? The way to do no harm to these pages was to do them the courtesy of listening to them.

I read the whole lot straight through, without making notes or trying to analyse. At the end of that reading, I decided not to make any more grand plans for the book. No more lists, no more attempts to see the shape of the whole thing. I'd start by making simple categories, and see where that led. I started with the biggest, simplest kind of rearrangement. I made two folders: 'London' and 'Australia'. Then I put the contents of each folder in what I thought might be chronological order.

The London material fell naturally into this structure.

Solomon Wiseman is born in the slums of Bermondsey. His childhood sweetheart, Sophia, is the daughter of a lighterman who takes Wiseman on as his apprentice. Solomon plans to marry Sophia as soon as his apprenticeship is over.

But his friend William Warner persuades him to go to the notorious Cherry Gardens with him and a couple of good-looking girls. Wiseman is swept up by one of them, Jane. She falls pregnant and Wiseman is forced to marry her.

Soon after, Warner marries Sophia—cynically, in hopes of inheriting her father's business. He is violent towards her, even breaks her jaw. Wiseman discovers this and gives Warner a savage beating.

Wiseman has always stolen from the loads he's carried. One night his employer—tipped off in advance by Warner, in revenge for the beating—catches him stealing some timber. He is tried and condemned to death, then to transportation for life. Jane is given permission to accompany him, and in 1806 they set sail for New South Wales.

I printed this out—a satisfying pile of about 80 pages—and put it away.

The folder called 'Australia' held about 140 pages. I did my best to put them into chronological order, too.

The Wisemans arrive in Sydney, Solomon gets a pardon, buys a boat, starts trading up and down the Hawkesbury. Against Jane's wishes they settle there.

There are various encounters with the Darug—some friendly, some hostile.

Wiseman plots a long-distance revenge on Warner. Through his brother, he arranges for Warner to be caught stealing. When Warner is transported, Solomon makes sure that his old rival is assigned to him. Unexpectedly, Sophia is also with him and the two couples live uncomfortably together for a time as masters and servants. Wiseman and Sophia resume their love affair in secret. But Jane humiliates and mistreats Sophia, so Wiseman arranges for Sophia and Warner to set up on land nearby.

Jane and Solomon argue continually about the 'blacks'— Jane is frightened of them and wants to go back to London. During one of their arguments he hits her and she falls down the stairs and is killed. Wiseman more or less buys Sophia from Warner and establishes her as his housekeeper. In due course Warner dies and Wiseman and Sophia marry. There are a few more meetings between settlers and Darug. As before, some are friendly, some are hostile.

After escalating attacks on both sides, a posse of settlers is organised. It combines with troops to form a Black Line to round up all the local Darug. The Black Line is a failure but later there's a massacre in which most of the Darug are killed. Then there's the bit about the fig tree and the rock.

I was pleased with this. None of my previous novels had much plot. That was all right—some of my favourite books had no plots to speak of. But I was proud of the fact that, with the story of Wiseman getting his revenge on Warner, I'd stumbled on a plot of almost operatic complexity. All it needed was a few cases of mistaken identity and a bit of cross-dressing.

Dividing things up seemed to be working, so I split the 'Australia' folder into two: one called 'White story' and one called 'Aboriginal story'.

With the meetings with Aboriginal people removed, 'White story' flowed much more smoothly.

'Aboriginal story' was more difficult. I found the same problem that Sturt did with those different tribes on the Murray. Sometimes the Aboriginal people were friendly to the Wisemans and sometimes they weren't, and I didn't understand why.

Still, I tried to make some kind of sequence. The scene based on that event with Governor Phillip, where an old man shows Wiseman a nice cosy cave to stay out of the rain: that went at the beginning, when things were friendly. The scene where the Aboriginal people burn an area of ground near the Wisemans' hut: it felt like a threat, so it went in the middle when things were becoming tense. The scene where a settler gets a spear through the stomach: that went at the end.

The two stories could be made to go smoothly on their own, but I couldn't find a way to knit them together. They bucked against each other like some clever bit of postmodernism.

It seemed to be a question of sequence. Should Wiseman discover that William Warner dobbed him in before or after he settles on the Hawkesbury? Should Jane die, and Wiseman marry Sophia Warner, before or after the Darug start the fire?

I made lists, I made lists in columns, I made summaries of each scene and wrote them on sticky notes that I rearranged on the window above the desk. I tried cutting the book into chapters, and gave each chapter a title. In desperation I got out my big scissors and cut the printout into sections. I was hoping that physically moving it might give me a new point of view. Then I stickytaped the bits together in a different order, with handwritten sections in between. This produced a weird-looking thing, bristling with frills and fringes.

I was panicking. I was working on the book at night now, and getting up at dawn at the weekends to rearrange things one more time. I even dreamt about it: myself on a launch on the Hawkesbury River, the water black, someone beside me not listening as I tried to explain that *we have to go back, we have to go back*. I woke up panting. Go back, where?

One night in October 2002, I went for my usual walk. I loved walking at night, even though it meant I had to stick to the well-lit streets. There was something about stepping out the front door into the dark, pulling it closed behind you, setting off down the street. I had some handweights that were supposed to be good for your arm muscles. I didn't know if they were, but they made you walk in a certain way—striding out. I had a good pair of walking shoes, plenty of bounce in the soles. I had a routine: swing out of the front door at eight-thirty, walk up to the pub at the roundabout and back, a good forty-minute workout.

It had been raining on and off all day, but now the rain had become hardly more than a mist. The drizzle made a radiant halo around every streetlight. Their reflections were bright blurs along the black road. I could feel the moisture settling in my hair, weighing it down, a drip starting down the side of my face. I could have brought an umbrella, but what did it matter, it was only water. As that Irishman in Tim Winton's book says, 'Afraid of a bit of soft weather then?'

After a few minutes I was warmed up and striding out. At the crossroads there was an ugly cairn, a bit too squat to be glorious, erected in honour of some past local worthy. His name was there in big carved letters: *THOMAS STEPHENSON ROWNTREE 1902.* I imagined them all standing around at the unveiling. Speeches. Women in big silly hats. Men in waistcoats and watch-chains. The friends and family of Thomas Rowntree, admiring his name carved in stone. *For ever*, they'd have thought. *They'll always remember him.*

Drops of water pattered in the fig trees around the cairn and I could hear fruit bats up in the branches. A spray of water came down as they made a bunch of leaves twitch. Poor old Thomas Rowntree, long forgotten. Only the fruit bats and the summer rain and this sweet cool air were still there.

I walked fast, feeling my feet springing along against the soles of my shoes. Past the video shop, where I waved hello to Amanda behind the counter. Past the hardware shop that always had a joke in its window. 'My wife uses the fire alarm as a timer.' Ha ha. Along the spooky bit where the streetlights were too far apart and the houses were always in darkness. Up to the pub at the roundabout, all those people laughing and shouting at each other and a cosy fug of beer smells leaking out the door, then turn back towards home.

I'd been in a pleasant moving trance with the rain on my skin and the footpath making a little wet sound at each step. I hadn't been thinking about anything at all, much less that recalcitrant book sitting on my desk.

So why was it that, at the moment I put my hand on the front gate to push it open, I saw exactly what I needed to do?

It was so simple. Get rid of William and Sophia Warner. Cut them out, kill them off.

Next morning, pen in hand, ready to cross out entire scenes, I could see what the problem was. I had two different stories in one book. One was a story about settlement—Wiseman and his family and their relationship with the Aboriginal people. The other was a classic revenge-and-romance story—Wiseman plotting over many years to square things with Warner and get Sophia.

I knew there was nothing wrong in principle with two stories in one book. But these two didn't make a happy marriage. The first was a sombre story based on real, tragic events. The second was a lightweight, contrived thing. Neither looked good in the light of the other. It was like eating steak and fairy floss together.

When it came to drawing a line through the words, though, and removing that part of the book, I couldn't seem to do it. Sophia was such a likeable character. That scene in the churchyard, where she and Wiseman had a cuddle, so moving. Perhaps I could make it work. One more list? One more lot of sticky notes on the window?

I remembered a trick I'd learned writing a previous book. I made a folder called 'Good Bits To Use Later'. I got out my big scissors again, literally cut Sophia and William Warner out, and put them into the folder. It was a grief to lose such a juicy plot, and the character of Sophia, but I knew it was a necessary sacrifice.

Straight away it was as if chains had dropped off the story. The Wisemans and the Aboriginal people were left alone to get

On the point of sleep,

It was so — like

A thought came to him that was as absurd ~~as the thought~~ of a dog opening its

~~Heart he put it away from him.~~

mouth and speaking ~~to him.~~ The thought ~~was this~~ that the black men were farmers no less

go to the labour of

than the white men ~~were.~~ The difference was ~~that~~ the blacks did not ~~bother to~~ build a fence

Let a little ... and simply ... to keep animals from getting out. Instead they ~~created~~ a patch ~~so tasty they lured them in~~ ... the animals to

Either way, the upshot was the same: fresh meat for dinner.

[make clear is it forest there or

so ... frenzy to clear?] replaced

start here   beyond the clearing

After breakfast, and after he had ...

Going on eight now, Dickie was too old to tether to the verandah-post. He would

and spent the day in ...

disappear by day into the hot dry ticking dream of the ~~bush~~ as if learning it by heart. He

look at

brought things back to the hut for them to ~~see:~~ a gum-leaf curled right around on itself like a

sleeping

dog ~~asleep,~~ a round white pebble, a piece of wood so eaten by the white-ants it had become

the other glanced briefly. Little Mary might marvel at the

a brown sponge. ~~He had taken to this new place as if it was the place he had always been~~

sleeping leaf, Will might ... the pebble for his slingshot but

waiting for   they would not have gone looking for them, ... would not have ...

~~Blackwood saw him sometimes~~ down by the river with the native children, all of

there more than once, around on the other side of the point — the blacks' side. He

had seen his Dickie there on a spit of sand like a beach, playing ... in the

stripped off like them to nothing but skin. His was white and theirs was black, but it seemed

out of the water, all ...

to Blackwood that the difference of skin did not amount to much. Running and laughing

sun, glistening with river-water, it ... hard to tell the difference. Dickie

with them, even ~~calling~~ out in their own words, he could have been their pale cousin.

should some of   on the wave ... 237

It filled ~~Sal~~ with a kind of panic. In kind of wail she said He's going to grow up a

(B) He could hear how

savage, he'll have forgot how to be civilised when we go home, her throat closed around her

In the end, to satisfy ... 237

desperation. In the end it seemed easier to go down to the blacks' camp to fetch him back

(A)   to (A) p 238

~~than weather her nagging.~~

B said nothing to Sal of what he saw, ...

~~It made it worse~~ pale boy who was happy not to go beyond the

clearing, gave the game away one day when Dickie ...

at sunset with wet hair and his ...

... but she did not miss much, even though she seemed ... never to look

beyond the yard ... somehow without telling Dickie

running and calling with the black children, she knew it was happening, and

---

The slash and burn approach to writing: try anything, and if it
doesn't work, try something else.

on with it, staring at each other up there on the Hawkesbury. It was just the two of them, working it out together, and that was what the story was. White meeting black, black meeting white, and everyone trying to decide what to do.

There were still plenty of problems to be solved, but for the first time since I started writing, nearly two years earlier, I thought I might have a novel.

23
Finding the Characters

I had a story, sort of. But who *were* these people? Why were they doing the things they did?

Solomon Wiseman was the biggest problem. If he wasn't a character, nothing else in the book would work. If I could get him right, perhaps I could fudge it a bit with some of the others.

Who was he? He was out of focus, the way he had been in all those letters and petitions he'd produced: sometimes reasonable, other times flying off the handle. And he was real. I was beginning to see that the powerful reality of Solomon Wiseman was part of the energy of this book, but it was also part of the problem. I was trying to incorporate everything that I'd found.

It felt a little disloyal to step back from my personal relationship with him, as if I was turning my back on a family member I'd only just discovered. I came to it in stages.

My relationship with him shifted the first time I found myself thinking of him not as 'Solomon Wiseman' but as 'the Wiseman character'. Using that form of words in my mind, and as it were avoiding his eye, I looked again at the scenes on the Hawkesbury, where his responses were so contradictory. Silently apologising to him, I came to see that there was a way of reconciling the contradictions. He begins with one way of thinking about the Aboriginal people, goes through several shifts of attitude, and ends up prepared to join an attack against them. By rearranging and reshaping the scenes, I could create a sequence.

This wasn't quite how it was in the documents, but making a sequence out of these scenes wouldn't distort what had 'really happened' in any significant way. It would, though, turn them into a story.

Now I could ask myself cold-bloodedly, 'What is the function of the Wiseman character in this story?' To answer that question I had to know what the central drama of the novel was, and now I could see it more clearly. It was the drama of watching a character make choices. The choices were to do with how to 'be' in the country he'd come to. That included his relationship with the place itself, as well as with the original inhabitants. The story was about the journey he takes in making his choices.

I'd written a number of scenes that I now saw had nothing to do with that central drama. They'd only ever been there because they 'really happened'. A lot of unconvincing stuff about his business affairs was one of the main things that went.

I didn't even bother with the 'Good Bits To Use Later' folder, just hit the delete button.

The suburb where we lived was nineteenth-century working-class turned gentrified. A few characters still hung on there, people born and bred when it was a school-of-hard-knocks shipbuilding suburb. We had one over our back fence: Old Mr Barnes. I had occasional conversations with him through the plumbago.

'How old d'you reckon I'd be?' he'd asked me several times.

I always pretended. 'Oh, seventy? Seventy-five?'

'Ninety-eight!' he crowed. 'Ninety-nine come June!'

After every shower of rain, Old Mr Barnes climbed up a ladder onto the roof of his kitchen—a corrugated iron lean-to on the back of his small house—with a paintbrush and a pot of black stuff. We'd offered to go up for him, but it was a matter of pride with him that he could still get up the ladder, still put another blob of stuff on the bit where the roof leaked.

He was up on his roof today, holding the paintbrush, looking as if he was enjoying the sun. When he caught sight of me getting the washing on the line he called out straight away, 'Bet you don't know how I got me nickname!'

'What nickname?'

It was when he was at school, he told me.

I tried to do the sums and work out what decade it would have been—even which century.

'There was this bigshot inspector come,' Mr Barnes called out. 'Wanted to know how you spelled island, well I told him. I-S-L-A-N-D. Dad worked at Garden Island, see.'

He dabbed the brush at the rusty bit of roof.

'So he says, "well done son, very sagacious of you."' Mr Barnes laughed so hard that I glimpsed his false teeth slip. 'We all think he's having a lend of me, but he says, sagacious means wise, son.'

With knobbed old hands he carefully squeezed the lid back on the tin of black stuff. 'So that's where it come from. Sagitty. Well, nice talking to you, Um.'

He turned himself around, very slowly, and explored with one foot for the rung of the ladder. I watched him, ready to leap through the plumbago, but he made it down all right. His foot had barely touched the ground when I was in the kitchen writing it down. 'Sagacious = Sagitty. Change all the names. Find nicknames.'

I knew just where to go for authentic late eighteenth-century names: the convict registers.

'Anty', a coal-heaver
John Blackwood
'Bully' Dawson
Thomas 'Hazzles' Herring
William Nettleship
John Ogle
'Birdy' Pidgeon
John Quick
William Thornhill
James Twist
William Underwood
'Scrummy' Williams

From 'the Wiseman character' it was a short step to William Thompson, then William Blackwood, then William Thornhill.

Changing his name changed my relationship to the character. My great-great-great grandfather had stepped out of the book now, taking his name with him. He had a story, the one I'd found in the archives, but it wasn't the one I was telling. He watched—sardonically, I felt—as I went on writing in another direction, further and further away from him.

I left Thornhill with Wiseman's quick temper, his tendency towards violence, and a certain cold-blooded determination. I gave him Wiseman's consciousness of humiliation by the gentry. I also gave him Wiseman's rough-and-ready sense of justice and even charity.

But in building a picture of Thornhill the family man, I went far beyond what I could guess about Wiseman. Thornhill's deep love for his wife, his softness with her, his love for his children—none of that came from the Wiseman I'd met in the archives.

Once that softer part of his personality was drawn in, the violence he might inflict on the Aboriginal people took on a different quality.

A man who wasn't altogether bad, but who did bad things, might feel something like remorse. That suggested a way the book might end—with Thornhill suspended between what he *was*, and what he'd *done*. He didn't have the insight to bring the two together, he was even hardly able to think about them, but he knew that something wasn't right.

Thornhill might have accepted that black people were not-quite-human 'savages'. On the other hand, being regarded as inferior within his own class system might have made him consider other kinds of 'inferiors' more sympathetically. His lack of education would have spared him knowledge of the pseudo-science that justified racism. And, as someone who spent a lot of time around the docks, he'd probably met and worked alongside foreign sailors of all colours and cultures. More than many of his educated contemporaries, he might have realised that difference doesn't mean inferiority.

When a man like that came into contact with the Aboriginal people in New South Wales, his response might have been pretty complex. I was starting to see that his attitude wouldn't be a fixed thing arrived at by education or thought, but more fluid, driven by day-to-day events.

It might be something quite personal that would tip the balance and make him decide to act in one way rather than another: something to do with his family, or his love for his wife. Not a considered attitude to Aboriginal people, just a pragmatic response to a problem.

And what about that wife? She'd always been a vaguer figure in my mind than Solomon. Partly this was because there'd been so little about Jane in the records. I'd tried to find out about her, but if the life of men on the frontier was hard to see at this distance of time, the life of women—especially of working-class women—was almost invisible.

As I'd written her so far, Jane was a permanently unhappy creature, wistful and sulky. That picture of her had drawn on the three things I knew about Jane Wiseman: the frequency of her pregnancies, her 'actual state of invalidity', and her 'lingering illness'.

Thinking about her now as 'the wife character' and giving

her another name—Sal—once again freed me from the strait-jacket of 'what really happened'. Her health improved miraculously but her temper grew worse. She hated the flies, the trees, the sun. She hankered for England. That was always 'Home'. Australia was one long punishment. Her husband bore the brunt of her outrage at what life had dumped on her.

The minor characters—the neighbours and the children—were so shallowly drawn that I considered getting rid of them altogether. Imagining the book without them showed me why I needed them. Settlement wasn't a matter of individual men and women acting simply out of their own personalities. It was about an entire world transplanted to the new place, bringing with it all the pressures and rewards it had always brought to bear on its members.

I saw—with a sinking heart, *how can I do this?*—that I would have to create a whole society on the riverside. Different individuals responded differently to the choices they had. Social pressures from those around him—loyalty, fear of exclusion, shame—as well as temperament would make Thornhill act in the way he did.

Smasher Farrell and Sagitty Birtles were already present, based on the barbarous settlers I'd read about. Blackwood—a defender of Aboriginal people—was there from the beginning, too. He'd emerged out of that mysterious place where characters sometimes come from, fully formed and complete. One day he even showed me what he looked like when I found a photo of Jack Mundey, the union leader, addressing a public meeting—a big solid man with a magnificent nose and a face full of powerful character. *Blackwood!* I thought. *So that's what you look like!*

I was shameless in rifling through research for anything I could use, wrenching it out of its place and adapting it for my own purposes: the man with a lump on the back of his neck from carrying bags of wheat; the gentleman down on his luck, proud of washing his own shirt; the man whose house was robbed by men who took everything, even the dinner on the fire—chicken, pot and all. But I was trying to be faithful to the shape of the historical record, and the meaning of all those events that historians had written about. What I was writing wasn't real, but it was as true as I could make it.

24

The Aboriginal Characters

Back in my student days I'd known a lighting designer who called himself Mr Fogg. We lost touch over the years, but I was somehow still on the mailing list for his irregular 'news-letter'. In the April 2003 edition, Mr Fogg told of a trip he'd made to the Kimberley in the remote north-west of Western Australia where he'd taken some photographs of a group of Aboriginal performers and artists. He'd exhibited the photos in Sydney and New York. Now he was going to take them back to the Kimberley and have some sort of exhibition there, so that the people in the photos could see themselves. Were there any sympathetic souls out there on his mailing list who'd like to join him?

I said yes.

I'd written scenes in which Thornhill deals with his Aboriginal neighbours, but I knew they weren't working. I'd never known anyone remotely like the Aboriginal characters I was describing, not even seen them from a distance. I was inventing them out of the only resources I had: stereotype, cliché and guesswork.

I'd always known I wasn't going to try to enter the consciousness of the Aboriginal characters. I didn't know or understand enough, and felt I never would. They—like everything else in the book—would be seen through Thornhill's eyes.

But Thornhill had one big advantage over his creator. He'd seen Aboriginal people, spoken to them, watched them going about their affairs. Heard them speak, seen their faces, their hands, their hair, their feet. I hadn't.

In any other novel, if I'd had that kind of difficulty with characters, I'd have left them out and written about ones I knew something about. But that day on the Sydney Harbour Bridge, meeting the eye of that woman, I'd seen that there was an empty space in my own family story where the Aboriginal people belonged. The whole point of writing this story was to fill that space.

More than that—to place them in the story so that they were as fully alive, as complex and as individual as the settlers. I didn't want them to be shadowy figures on the edge of the action or stereotypes.

I didn't want to try to get inside the Aboriginal characters, but I needed to see what Thornhill would have: people of unmixed Aboriginal descent, living in traditional ways.

The Kimberley had cars and supermarkets, but it was the closest I was likely to come to seeing what he had seen.

In the end there were seven 'sympathetic souls' along for the ride with Mr Fogg: a minibus full of old hippies.

We arrived in Kununurra, the main town in the Kimberley, in the afternoon. We were staying out at the caravan park, so we went to the supermarket first for supplies. Waiting for the others outside, I was staring around. The light was so white, the shadows so solid. The sky so pale. Everything was new.

I wasn't far from a group of Aboriginal people talking among themselves. Their skin was as black as the shadows. Their faces—I glanced quickly and then away—folded in on themselves, unreadable. They were talking quietly, and at first I thought that was why I couldn't hear what they were saying. Then I realised they weren't speaking English. They were speaking a language where all the words and even the cadences were unlike anything I'd heard before.

Oh, I thought to myself, *they're speaking a foreign language.*

I heard myself think that thought.

No, I realised. *It's me. I'm the one speaking the foreign language.*

I was ashamed. My first reaction had been to think they were the foreigners. That was how backward I was, underneath those fine sentiments. In spite of all my good intentions and my high-minded thoughts, I didn't understand a thing.

Now *that* was something I was never going to learn from a book. But I could use it. Thornhill might have reacted in just the same way.

Groups of Aboriginal people sat under the trees in the parks of Kununurra, blending into the flickering light and shade. The sounds of their laughter carried across the grass to us. They had an ability to do nothing more than sit. Even in full sun the details of their faces somehow disappeared. They always looked cross—those heavy frowning brows, those serious mouths—until they smiled. Then you could see they weren't angry. It was just the way their faces were.

One man sat alone under a tree, so still, as if he was listening to something, tuned in to some other place. The darkness of his face made it impossible to read his expression.

Another man walked across the grass towards us, heading for the shop. He shot a quick glance our way and a spot of reflected light flicked into his eyes from a passing car. It made them so bright in the darkness of his face that it was as if they were lit from within.

When the Aboriginal people walked, it was in a way no European walked—it was leisurely, but they seemed to cover the ground fast. They were all legs: long thin legs with no bulging calf muscle, the feet big boxy shapes. Their bare feet settled down into each deliberate step, their weight somehow carried behind the hips. Even in the white glare of noon in Kununurra, when all humans became nothing more than silhouettes, it was easy to tell a white person from a black one by the way they moved.

I passed an old man sitting crosslegged on the ground, a wiry grey beard, Einstein hair, a black vest on his bare chest. 'Hello,' I said as I passed—it seemed rude to say nothing—and he gave a small gesture with one hand and an inclination of the head: a king acknowledging his subject.

When they looked at us what did they see? Did they think, *our land, these rude people coming without asking?* We might have seen them as 'homeless' or what a shopkeeper called 'riffraff'—but did they regard us as people who'd walked straight into their living room without even knocking?

Nothing was disturbing or threatening about any of them,

but there was a powerful sense of them as 'other'. For a man like Thornhill, out there in the bush, a day's boat ride from any help, that otherness might have seemed threatening. He might have been frightened, and fear might have made him do anything at all.

We met the artists at the house where they stayed when they were in town. They were old men in frayed suit jackets, flannelette shirts, bare feet. They were stern, dignified. Their faces were on a big scale. Nose, eyebrows, mouth: everything was large, serious, workmanlike.

They didn't speak much. Their English was so accented it was almost impossible to understand. It came in clots, short bursts of sound. My Gija, however, was much worse than their English.

Even with each other they seemed to be men of few words.

One man sat on the couch on the verandah. With a long imperious finger he gestured for his cup to be refilled—a flick of the wrist, a small expressive movement of the shiny black fingers, fluid as water, as if they were equipped with extra joints.

They were cattlemen before the equal pay claim went through in 1968. Then they were all sacked by the station owners. But it meant these men knew their country, because the cattle stations were on their traditional land. That was what they painted. The canvases were simple shapes in bold colours, a few lines of dots. Some of them had terse titles. 'Kangaroo Dreaming'. 'Emu Dreaming'. Now and then, if pressed, they might reluctantly point to a part of the painting and say, 'it's a big waterhole' or 'where the emu went'.

You knew it was much more than a big waterhole, much more than a symbolic shape on canvas. It embodied the whole story they knew about the place. They knew the story in all its nuances, but they were only going to tell what they chose to.

They painted with total absorption. What they were seeing as they painted seemed to go far beyond the surface of the canvas. It was as if they could see every detail of the place in the eye of their mind, even though it might have been years since they'd been able to visit it. Watching them paint you could see how deep it went. They didn't need to see it.

I felt awkward with them. Not easily sharing a language made it difficult. But it was more than that. These rigorous old men made me aware that I was living in a place I didn't know the first thing about.

We had the show in the Kununurra library. The librarian told me the men had probably never been inside the library before. She was terribly pleased that they were there and understood that it wouldn't have been easy for them to come. They stalked in as a group, in cowboy shirts and boots, courteous but reserved, and sat down in the plastic chairs, their faces unreadable.

An elder from their community gave a speech. She stood four-square, in a bright patterned skirt and a shirt of another bright pattern. Her face was lean, deeply grooved. Her face, her body, had nothing extraneous about them. The essential human face, the essential human body.

She told the story of a massacre of Aboriginal people that had happened on their country. A boab tree marked the spot. After the massacre the bodies were burned. She told us that there was still a big bare place on the ground. 'The fat came out of the bodies,' she said, very matter-of-fact. 'So nothing grows there after that.'

The audience—mostly white—listened in silence. In this

welcoming place, this room full of books, pictures, smiling librarians, this story was like a truck driving through the wall. The things she was talking about had happened just down the road. It was in the lifetime of her own grandmother. Of our own grandmothers.

Afterwards, when everyone had gone, we took down the white fabric we'd pinned up as background for the photographs and put the chairs back where they belonged. I moved the chair where one of the painters had sat, a long tall thin man with legs bowed as if from years in the saddle. On the carpet around the chair were pebbles—red chips of the stone the country was made of.

The librarian saw them too. Her eyes met mine. 'He brought them in with him,' she said. She was almost whispering. 'I saw him get them out of his pocket.' She made a secretive twisting gesture with a hand down near her hip. 'Dropped them all around him.'

We stared at each other. Like me, she was from 'down south'. We didn't know what this was about, these bits of the country brought into the foreign place of the library. But we knew it was something. The gaudy shirt, the swaggering gait in the boots—all that was surface decoration, laid on top of something else.

Back in Sydney, I made some decisions. I would get rid of all the Aboriginal dialogue. It might be historically accurate to have the Aboriginal characters speaking broken English, but it made them less sympathetic, more caricatured.

Their inside story—their responses, their thoughts, their feelings—all that was for someone else to tell, someone who had the right to enter that world and the knowledge to do it properly.

I might not be able to enter the Darug consciousness, but I could make it clear that there *was* one. To create a hollow in the book, a space of difference that would be more eloquent than any words I might invent to explain it. To let the reader know that a story was there to be told, but not to try to tell it.

Around about the same time I began to realise that the Aboriginal people were emerging in a way I hadn't planned: through the descriptions of landscape. The rocks, the trees, the river—I realised that I was often describing them in human terms—the golden flesh of the rocks beneath their dark skin, the trees gesturing, the bush watchful and alive. Humanising the landscape could be a way of showing the link between indigenous people and their land because, in some way that I recognised without really understanding, the country *was* the people.

I had one other problem in depicting the Darug: I needed the reader to be aware of things about the Aboriginal people that Thornhill wouldn't have known—the importance of those yam daisies, for example. How was I going to convey them without intruding too obviously into Thornhill's point of view?

Once or twice I used another character, usually Blackwood, to explain things to Thornhill. But I knew it could sound phoney to have one character explaining something to another, how it could break the trance of reading. Draft by draft I removed scenes where Blackwood held forth, and kept only a very few. Even those felt laboured, but they were so important I had to leave them.

One or twice I let Thornhill work things out for himself, as part of the journey of his thinking. For example, after seeing the Aboriginal strategy for burning the grass to attract game, he glimpses the idea that this is a kind of farming. I could get away with this a couple of times, but more than that and Thornhill would start to be too good to be true.

25
Dialogue

Somewhere or other I'd heard an ancient recording of the nineteenth-century poet Robert Browning. He was at some kind of celebration, it sounded like, and someone had brought along this new-fangled thing with a wax cylinder, and they wanted him to recite one of his poems into the horn. 'I sprang to the saddle, and Joris and he; I galloped, Dirck galloped, we galloped all three.' His voice was excited, light, uncertain, full of laughter. He sounded so astonishingly like us. He stumbled, stopped. He'd forgotten the rest. 'I'm incredibly sorry,' he called out, 'but I can't remember.' He laughed, and that was it.

So you could hear—sort of—what Robert Browning sounded like. But who would have brought along a wax cylinder to some hovel in Bermondsey and got an illiterate lighterman to speak into it? Even if the wax cylinder had been invented?

I wanted to create convincing dialogue. If I were writing about polite middle-class parlours I'd have been all right— I could have extrapolated from Jane Austen. But trying to think how people would have spoken in Bermondsey in the late eighteenth century, all that came to mind were a few novels in which working people made brief appearances: books by Defoe, Fielding, Sterne. Dickens did the lower orders, of course, but he was a good half-century later.

I could guess the limitations of these sources. The language they put into their characters' mouths was *their* version of how working people spoke. They'd have cleaned it up, perhaps unconsciously, to make it fit for their genteel, educated readership. Like Henry Humpherus, they might refer to 'foul oaths', but they never wrote the oaths down.

Writing those first drafts, and thinking of how to convey the harsh, uneducated quality of the characters, I'd made every second word of their dialogue 'fucken'. It was all 'fucken' this and 'fucken' that.

It had done the job—it got that first draft written. But, even as I was writing, I knew I hadn't got it right. I had made the dialogue sound coarse, but at the same time too modern and too monotonous.

The closest we were ever going to get to the wax cylinder of Robert Browning, I thought, was the transcripts of the Old Bailey trials. I went back to the Reading Room at the Mitchell Library and crouched over the microfilm reader, writing down phrases as they'd fallen from the lips of the criminal class two hundred years before.

I had a kick over the knee by a bullock
Damn my eyes
There is a man killed
Get off of it
You bugger
Give it them directly
Sixpenny worth
Damn you Jack

I was lucky enough to have some expert help researching eighteenth-century vernacular. On the matter of Dickens' use of Cockney it seemed that scholars were divided. Some thought that he'd exaggerated its quaintness (that 'werry' for 'very' was thought by some to be invention), and Dickens too had drawn a veil over foul oaths. I stole a few things, though: 'I gave him a souse across the chops', 'shut your bone-box'.

Cockney had changed radically since Wiseman's day (in part because of all those Weissmanns who arrived in the nineteenth century), but just the same I made lists of words and phrases I thought I might be able to use:

He axed me
Arse about face
Had a bellyful of that
There ain't nuffink like it
Gawdelpus
Wotcher (ie, what cheer)
Give us it
Dressed any old how

Some of these—'dressed any old how', for example—were things I'd heard Mum say, and they made me remember other things I'd heard from her, and from her father: 'when all's said and done', 'by and by', 'done us proud', 'my word', 'donkey's years', 'I'll do it directly', 'as plain as the nose on your face'.

Grandfather's old-fashioned country phrases reminded me of kids I'd gone to school with. They'd said things like: 'Are youse coming?', 'I never' (meaning 'I didn't'), 'I like her, but' (meaning 'I like her, though'), 'You was dobbed'.

Thinking about Aboriginal speakers of English I'd heard, I realised that they used English in some subtly different ways. The word 'gammon' (meaning humbug or fooling) for instance—it sounded as if it could be a remnant of eighteenth- and nineteenth-century English preserved in Aboriginal idiom. In any case I used it.

Private letters and journals generally weren't much use because they were written by people more educated than Thornhill. They'd have been cleaned up, too. But I looked through some and scavenged a few things. The letters of Mary Reiby, for example, gave me a few nice phrases—'the necessaries' (meaning 'the toilet'), 'I will watch every opportunity to get away in 2 years', 'I have near a hundred pounds about me', 'I am never without a box of tea in the house'.

Having gathered all these, of course I had to use them. Early drafts bristled with those colourful turns of phrase. Characters were forever threatening to give each other 'a souse across the chops' or were having 'a bellyful' of something or other.

It began to sound like a ye olde parody.

By the end of 2003 I was weeding out the most self-consciously picturesque idioms. Each phrase had to pass two tests. Did it scream smart-alec research? Was the meaning clear to a modern reader?

The 'antique' words I left in were those where the meaning was clear and which were reasonably familiar, if only from literature ('physick', 'apothecary', 'britches') or still used today, although unusual ('rotgut', 'tucker', 'victuals').

I also had to decide whether I wanted to spell words phonetically, as some of those lists had ('Gawdelpus', 'nuffink'), to suggest how they were pronounced.

When I tried this it made the speaker into a member of some quaint group whose language had laboriously to be spelled out. It implied that the writer (and reader) were the standard from which these other speakers deviated.

You couldn't really take a character seriously—in the sense of identifying with them and sharing their feelings—if you had to mouth out some oddly spelled version of how they were talking.

Of course, if the whole book was written in some kind of 'dialect'—like *A Clockwork Orange* or *Huckleberry Finn*—it became the standard language rather than a peculiarity, and the reader soon adjusted.

I was wrestling with all this when I happened to hear E. Annie Proulx talking on the radio. She said that she tried to make the order of the words convey the 'accent' or cadence, rather than spelling it all out phonetically. She used turns of speech and vocabulary that were distinctive to the characters, but sparingly. Sometimes she did use phonetic spellings, but only when it was a word we'd got used to seeing spelled that way—like 'git' for 'get'. A scattering of phonetic spellings and a lot of work on the rhythm of the sentence would give you an accent more seamlessly, she thought, than all that tedious stuff with apostrophes.

Thank you, Annie Proulx.

With relief I got rid of 'fucken' and almost all of the other phonetic spellings, leaving only a few common ones such as 'ain't'. At last I decided that my job as a novelist wasn't to reconstruct the authentic sound of nineteenth-century vernacular. My job was to produce something that *sounded* authentic. No Thames waterman was going to rise up from between the lines and accuse me of getting it wrong.

And if he did, I'd be taking notes.

Around November 2003, I read all the dialogue aloud. If anything hit a false note, it was obvious straight away. This was a bad one, for example: 'That bit of land, he said. Remember I told you. We'll lose it if we don't move soon.'

This sounded terribly drawing-room. I muddied it up: 'That bit of land, he said. Remember I telled you. We'll miss out if we don't grab it.'

I deleted yards and yards of dialogue. This scene, for example, had made heavy weather of its speeches:

There was a meeting, Mrs Devine said. Oh my very word yes. A meeting and that. Just down here a piece, on the boat, he come up on the boat. They all got on, all the blacks, got on the boat and met the Governor, see.

She was knitting fast and faster, not looking at him, watching the wool fly between her fingers, the needles four pieces of nail-wire, waxed and gleaming from the grease in the wool. And not long enough, so she had to keep her eyes on what she was doing so the stitches would not fall off the end. There was one of the blacks, had a splattering of English, she said, and stopped knitting to count the stitches. Anyway the upshot was, the Governor promised them, no more farms down the river, no more down from Green's or Grono's, round about there.

No more? No more farms on the river? All that good land?

He did not believe.

You don't believe me, she said tartly, you ask my Da.

Why, he said. Why your Da.

He were there on the boat, weren't he? she shot back. He were a lumper on the *Liberty* and he were coiling a rope, he sez, and listening.

She looked up at him and laughed so he saw the two yellow teeth stuck in her bottom jaw like nails round a hogshead from which the top had been levered.

No one sees a lumper, that's what he sez. She shook her head.

No one sees a lumper, nor yet an old chook of an old woman.

At half the length it had some hope of working, although I was sad to lose those nail-wire knitting needles.

Blackwood, not taking his eyes off the cliffs, rode over Sagitty as if he had not spoken. There was a meeting, he said. Governor come up on the *Porpoise*, anchored off the point there. His head jerked to indicate the place. There was one of the blacks had a bit of English. His thick fingers were carefully rewinding the whipping on a bit of rope and he seemed to be talking to the cord rather than the people around him. Upshot of it was, Governor said there'd be no more white fellers downstream of the Second Branch.

You're lying, Tom Blackwood, Sagitty shouted, but

Blackwood calmly knotted up the whipping and snipped it off with his teeth. Shook hands, the lot, he said. That's how it was.

As a kid, I had some decided ideas about how books should be written. I thought, for example, they should have toilets in them. People in real life went to the toilet, so how come people in books never did? And I thought that when people talked in books it shouldn't be on a new line, indented, between quotation marks. Real life didn't stop dead while people talked, so why should it in books?

In other novels I'd tried different devices to let dialogue be part of the flow of the moment, rather than quarantined from it. I'd tried starting a new line, and I'd tried introducing dialogue with a dash. I'd tried using single quotation marks and no new line. I'd also tried italics.

In the first eight or ten drafts of *The Secret River* I did nothing more than make sure the dialogue was attached to a 'he said' or 'she said'. But there was always the danger that a reader mightn't immediately know whether something was dialogue or narrative. It also meant that dialogue could never be more than one sentence long.

Some time in the beginning of 2004, the dialogue went into italics. It solved some problems, but created others. More than a line or so of italics is irritatingly hard to read, so my dialogue had to stay short. And I couldn't use italics for anything else. This made difficulties if something that was normally italicised—the name of a boat, for instance—occurred in the dialogue.

After having wrestled with the voices of my characters for several years, another truth about writing was beginning to make itself known to me. Not only should you never have a blank page, and not only could you encourage yourself with the reminder that you could fix it up later. You also had to accept that *the solution to every problem creates another.*

26

The First Readers

It's no good asking friends and family to read your manuscript. If they say they love it, you don't believe them. If they have criticisms, it stings. It puts friends in an awkward position if they hate it, and it's asking a lot of anyone to give up the amount of time it takes to read a manuscript and think about it.

But in the middle of 2004 I laid this burden on several friends and on my husband. They read the manuscript, they made notes, and they talked about it with me.

They all liked the book (or they said they did). They had a list of queries, suggestions, insights. Two Aboriginal readers, Melissa Lucashenko and John Maynard, pointed out in the most tactful way that didgeridoos (described at enthusiastic length) wouldn't have been seen around Sydney, since originally they were used only by Arnhem Land people.

But they all agreed on one thing: Sal wasn't working.

They put it in different ways. 'Sal's character needs a bit of development.' 'Sal needs to be more interesting.' 'Beef up Sal a bit.'

They were right, I agreed with them, and I appreciated their frankness. I looked at the scenes they pointed to and tried to develop Sal along the lines they suggested. I extended some of her scenes. I gave her more dialogue. I worked out what she looked like, what she wore—the ragged fringe on her shawl, the patched bonnet. I gave her likes and dislikes, had her plant geraniums and yearn for nice teacups.

It all helped. But when I gave the book to its publisher, Michael Heyward, for the first time, in March 2004, Sal still wasn't working. I didn't know what else to do.

All my previous novels had had fine editors who'd suggested changes for the sake of pace, consistency or clarity and caught my errors of fact, grammar and punctuation. The publishers who employed them had reassured me that the books needed only 'a light edit' and had scheduled accordingly. I'd enjoyed working with those editors and valued all that they'd added.

But for one novel—*Dark Places*—I'd had a session with the publisher Hilary McPhee, then at Macmillan. We met only once, and hardly looked at the text. Instead we'd had a conversation that allowed me to see what sort of thing the book was and what it was doing, and what changes could be made to allow it to be more itself.

That experience told me what I'd always suspected: that an editor and a writer could together do something more than a 'light edit'. I was hoping to find that again with my new publisher.

Michael told me he was doing a 'broad-brush read-through'. Then in June 2004 we got together across my agent's dining-room table and did what he called 'turning the pages'.

I hadn't worked with Michael before. The first surprise was how little he'd written on the manuscript. Like Hilary with *Dark Places*, Michael hadn't burrowed into the words—that would come later in rigorous detail—but into the meaning of the book and its characters.

We turned quickly through as far as page 78, where Thornhill and Sal have recently arrived in Sydney. On this page he'd written 'Sal has changed'. He explained what he meant. The Sal we meet in London is happy, tender, playful, but as soon as she arrives in Sydney she's moody, grumpy, a nag. Thornhill notices it too:

> Since those days when they had listened to each other's stomachs rumble in Butler's Buildings, Sal had become a different creature…her face had a beaten look now, her cheeks sallow. Her voice was squeezed of all its laughter. In this Sal he could recognise nothing of the other Sal, her face soft in the candlelight at the table, the pucker between her eyebrows as she dotted out the letters from him to trace. At times, the sudden thought of that Sal pierced him like a light shining out in a dark night.

It was plausible that a nine-month voyage into exile would change a woman. But the change had all happened off-stage, between pages 74 and 75. That made for a very bumpy and unsatisfying experience for the reader.

That was straightforward enough, and I was scribbling notes as he talked. *Change too abrupt. Show change. Smooth transition.* I was still thinking of it as a technical problem.

But then Michael said, 'in the London scenes you've got an opportunity to complicate her later grumpiness, and I saw that this was an invitation to walk into the book and look around—not as a plumber come to fix the pipes, but as an architect seeing what else you might do with the space.

We turned through the pages together, and it was as if Michael's comments were a map of the book I'd written: not suggestions, but a sketch of what was there: 'Sal dislocated, cannot recognise home. Sal tough about Scabby Bill. Sal diminished.' The architect was being given a plan of the place, with the windows drawn in and the height of the ceiling given.

He used the word 'darken' to suggest what might be done to Sal's character in London. The word worked like the opening of a door: I could see the space beyond it, and suddenly couldn't wait to enter it, see what was there, do things with it.

What an astonishing thing memory is. It must have been over forty years since I'd read *Black Beauty* by Anna Sewell—up in that treehouse, a piece of forbidden chocolate probably melting in my fingers, a glass of milk threatening to tip over as the branches heaved in the wind. I'd never thought about it since. Kids didn't seem to read *Black Beauty* these days.

But feed the idea of 'darkening Sal' into the mysterious machinery of the unconscious, and out came that scene in *Black Beauty* where a man whips a horse that's fallen down in the street.

I remembered the effect that scene had on me. I'd had a sheltered childhood, had never experienced that kind of cruelty. But the writing must have been vivid enough for me to believe that the world contained people like that man. I learned something about life, even though it was nothing more than made-up words on a page, and it stayed in my memory for all those years. I didn't go back and read it now, but used my memory of it—whether accurate or not—as the trigger to free-associate about Sal:

> She was a soft-hearted little thing: had set upon a big hulk of a man whose horse had buckled at the knees but who went on labouring at him with a stick to make him rise. *Stop, leave off!* she had shrilled, and beat her small fists on his great back. *Leave off!* and the man had shrugged her off like a kitten and would have turned the stick on her, except that Thornhill pulled her away.

Thank you, Anna Sewell.

Michael didn't know about Sophia, still patiently waiting in the 'Good Bits To Use Later' folder. But standing in the space offered to me by the idea of 'darkening' Sal, I realised that I could adapt some of that material. Sophia had been an attractive character (hence painful to lose) because the sweetness of her nature always had a darker side. She had known the deaths of many brothers and sisters. Had nearly died from smallpox and was scarred by it. Understood something of fear and grief.

It felt as though Sophia was always meant to be the London Sal, but I hadn't realised that until now. My pleasure in the complicated revenge plot, and my disappointment at it not working, had prevented me from understanding her real place in the book. Being invited to think about Sal afresh allowed me to see the way I'd tried to force the story into the shape I thought it should have. I'd got in its way.

Now I could make use of what earlier readers had said. One of them had pointed to a specific scene where I might 'beef up' Sal's character—an episode in which Sal's mother and father die and she and Thornhill are plunged into poverty. I planned to add a couple of paragraphs. Six pages later, it was starting to look as though this new, darker Sal was at least as strong as her husband. She might have even been stronger. Much more likely to become that fierce person in Australia.

But Michael had something else to say about that Australian Sal. He had gone cautiously, in case I got sensitive about being criticised. He put it like this: 'Once Sal gets the glooms, there's nowhere for her to go.'

Of course! That was why she was boring. She gets off the boat in Sydney a screeching harridan and she's still screeching two hundred pages later. Having changed too radically between London and Sydney, she then doesn't change at all.

That would be boring in life, and it was boring in a book too.

Sal needed what her husband had acquired—a sequence. A journey.

Again there was that feeling that I was being offered a space where I could go on exploring. There was still time to do much more than tinker with adverbs. I could get to know Sal, as I'd got to know Thornhill, by putting her in situations and watching what she did. The book wasn't finished yet.

I went back to the scene of the Wisemans' arrival in Sydney, when they'd been approached by an Aboriginal man:

She took a step forward and shooed him off as you would a chook that had strayed into the house, *Go on! Bugger off!* Shooing at him close enough that Thornhill flinched, expecting her hand to strike the man, and then what would happen?

She was eyeball-to-eyeball with the black man. *This is our place*, she mouthed loudly. *Belongs to us now*.

The man started to speak, but Sal was out-shouting him, *Bugger off you dirty poxy savage with your mumbo-bloody-jumbo*, she was shrieking, and turned savagely to Thornhill, *come on Will you scared of this savage, you going to let him rule the roost, leave it all to me, where are your bloody balls Will? You got to take a firm line, from the start, like you do with a pup.*

I put the new Sal into the moment, started to write, and watched what she did.

What does he want, our victuals is it, Sal whispered, as if the fellow would not hear if she whispered.

Thornhill gave the man the shred of meat, but it was not that he wanted. They were all stuck in the moment. Thornhill could hear Sal breathing somewhat heavily beside him, as if preparing to fight. But when she spoke her voice was a little uncertain. *What does he want, Will? If it ain't the victuals?*

Her uncertainty, the fear in her voice, made Thornhill bold.

He took a step forward so he was eyeball-to-eyeball with the man.

Bugger off, he shouted. *Bugger off!*

He could hear his voice harsh, loud in the quiet dusk. He made shooing gestures, like you would shoo a chook that had got into the house.

After a long moment, the man turned and walked away around the rise of the slope.

Sal was crying, sniffing, gulping. *I am scared, Will, they are gunna spear us.*

Thornhill thought that too, imagined the blacks coming back with others, all those spears.

Bullshit, Sal, he said, *they're savages, you just got to take a firm line from the start, like you do with a pup.*

This still wasn't publishable, but it was better. This Sal was more consistent with the London Sal, and she was frightened rather than bullying. That gave her leeway to travel somewhere emotionally.

The big surprise was the way that Thornhill took over some of the old Sal's lines. They suited him better than her. His character was shifting, too.

As I rewrote scene after scene, I realised that the 'broad-brush' conversation with Michael was allowing me to become once again a person who *created* writing rather than a person who *analysed* it. In writing the first draft, I'd been exploring, writing into the unknown, trusting the unconscious and using free association as the mechanism by which it could speak. Once that first draft was down, I'd shifted gear, trying to understand and refine what I'd done. Both processes were necessary. But Michael had relieved me of the job of analysis and criticism, and invited me instead to go back into the unconscious. Now, right at the end, my job was as it had been in the beginning: not primarily to understand what I was doing, but to travel forward into it.

27
Into the World

It was the end of the day, April 2005. I'd just sent Michael the last changes on the last set of proofs. We'd worked hard together, and discussed every sentence in detail. Now I stood at my desk, aimlessly moving pieces of paper into piles. The frantic notes to myself, the lists of changes, the mail that had gone unanswered, even unopened, during this last race to the finish-line: I jumbled it all together and put it on one side of the desk.

It was over. Next time I saw those words I'd written, they'd be a bound book. Too late for any more thoughts.

It should have been a joyful moment, but it was an anti-climax, even something like panic: a gap in my life where this book had been for the last five years. *What now? What do I do now?*

Outside, the sun had set but it wasn't quite dark. I couldn't bear that desk, that window with the yellow sticky notes all over it, that lamp, that laptop, for one more moment.

That good feeling, calling out to Bruce that I was going for a walk, swinging out the door and pulling it closed. Out the front gate, along the footpath.

I was heading downhill tonight. Down to the park and the harbour instead of up the hill towards the pub. It was probably not as safe, but it was nicer, and there was still a bit of light in the sky to frighten away the rapists.

As soon as I reached the park the air changed. It was like walking from a small room into a huge open atrium. Sounds could go further before they bounced back. I could smell the harbour: salt, seaweed, diesel. A sense of water restless in its bed of land.

It was high tide. The water swelled up sumptuously against the weed-streaming planks of the dock, tossed a wave at the sea wall, broke into foam. It was like something living: turning under and over, through and along, dancing with itself. It caught the light from all around, the surface reflecting the lamps along the dock, the glowing honeycombs of the apartments, the flashing signals on the mooring-posts further out. The coloured surface of the water—restless patterns of orange, of red, of white—slid over the satin blackness underneath.

Straight across the water, so close I felt it would only be a few strokes of freestyle, was a bulk of land, a headland on the opposite shore. Above it was the sky, holding the last glow of sunset. Below, the water taking the light in from anywhere and making its own artwork from it. In between, this solid mass of darkness.

It was too steep to build on, so they made it a park: all rock ledges, cliff-faces, the grass that cuts your hands if you grab it to stop yourself falling. Up on the top, on an open platform, a big fish was engraved in the rock.

They'd walked us down from North Sydney Demonstration School to see that engraving. It was beside the road, behind a white council fence. The grooved image had been filled in with a thick white line of high-gloss paint, making it crude, lifeless, utterly unlovely.

We hung over the fence, glanced, ticked the box on our Excursion Sheet—*Aboriginal Engraving*—and turned away.

Ball's Head, that promontory was called now. It was named after Lieutenant Ball, a marine with the First Fleet. One tiny fact in all that reading I'd done. It was so easy to imagine them: the boat with the oars dipping in and out of the water, making its way under the great prow of the headland. Two or three bays back were the eleven ships of the fleet, the thousand souls free and convict, the piano brought along by George Worgan the surgeon, the bags of rice and flour.

And watching them, the others.

The people who had another name for Ball's Head. The people who scraped out the groove of the fish every year so it was always bright, and who would have had a story about it that they taught their children.

While Lieutenant Ball and the others were working their way around the headland, there were people watching them. Standing, probably, more or less where I was now, down at the water's edge, looking across at the headland and the boat under it.

Behind them, there'd have been a creek running down a little valley. The valley floor had been filled in and flattened now to accommodate the oval and the public toilets. There'd have been rock ledges and overhangs on the steep valley walls on both sides. In summer they'd have used the ones on the south-facing slope. That was posh Louisa Road now. They'd stay cool, they'd get the breeze. In winter they'd have wanted the warmth of the sun, and gone over to the rock shelters that faced north. The backyards still tumble down the slope, every house looking over the head of the one in front.

I'd laughed with the other kids at that fish up on Ball's Head. All I could see then were the wharves and buildings, the streets, the glitter and bulk of the things that were on the surface of the place that was my home.

Writing *The Secret River* was the opening of a new set of eyes in my head, a new set of ears. Now I could see what was underneath, what was always underneath and always will be: the shape of the land, the place itself, and the spirit of the people who were here.

Acknowledgments

Many people helped me in the writing of *The Secret River*. A few of you are mentioned specifically in these pages but most are not. Please, all of you, accept here my gratitude for the talking, thinking, lending of books, supplying of information, reading of drafts, guiding, encouraging and challenging that you did. This book is the record of the journey on which you all accompanied me, and which couldn't have happened without you.

The novel inspired by Kate Grenville's journey in
Searching for the Secret River

The Secret River

Shortlisted for the 2006 Man Booker Prize
Winner of the 2006 Commonwealth Writers' Prize

London, 1806 – William Thornhill, happily wedded to his childhood sweetheart Sal, is a waterman on the River Thames. Life is tough but bearable until William makes a mistake, a bad mistake for which he and his family are made to pay dearly. His sentence: to be transported to New South Wales for the term of his natural life. Soon Thornhill, a man no better or worse than most, has to make the most difficult decision of his life . . .

The *Alexander*, with its cargo of convicts, had bucked over the face of the ocean for the better part of a year. Now it had fetched up at the end of the earth. There was no lock on the door of the hut where William Thornhill, transported for the term of his natural life in the Year of Our Lord eighteen hundred and six, was passing his first night in His Majesty's penal colony of New South Wales. There was hardly a door, barely a wall: only a flap of bark, a screen of sticks and mud. There was no need of lock, of door, of wall: this was a prison whose bars were ten thousand miles of water.

Thornhill's wife was sleeping sweet and peaceful against him, her hand still entwined in his. The child and the baby were asleep too, curled up together. Only Thornhill could not bring himself to close his eyes on this foreign darkness. Through the doorway of the hut he could feel the night, huge and damp, flowing in and bringing with it the sounds of its own life: tickings and creakings, small private rustlings, and beyond that the soughing of the forest, mile after mile.

When he got up and stepped out through the doorway there was no cry, no guard: only the living night. The air moved around him, full of rich dank smells. Trees stood tall over him. A breeze shivered through the leaves, then died, and left only the vast fact of the forest.

He was nothing more than a flea on the side of some enormous quiet creature.

Down the hill the settlement was hidden by the darkness. A dog barked in a tired way and stopped. From the bay where the *Alexander* was anchored there was a sense of restless water shifting in its bed of land and swelling up against the shore.

Above him in the sky was a thin moon and a scatter of stars as meaningless as spilt rice. There was no Pole Star, a friend to guide him on the Thames, no Bear that he had known all his life: only this blaze, unreadable, indifferent.

All the many months in the *Alexander*, lying in the hammock which was all the territory he could claim in the world, listening to the sea slap against the side of the ship and trying to hear the voices of his own wife, his own children, in the noise from the women's quarters, he had been comforted by telling over the bends of his own Thames. The Isle of Dogs, the deep eddying pool of Rotherhithe, the sudden twist of the sky as the river swung around the corner to Lambeth: they were all as intimate to him as breathing. Daniel Ellison grunted in his hammock beside him, fighting even in his sleep, the women were silent beyond their bulkhead, and still in the eye of his mind he rounded bend after bend of that river.

Now, standing in the great sighing lung of this other place and feeling the dirt chill under his feet, he knew that life was gone. He might as well have swung at the end of the rope they had measured for him. This was a place, like death, from which men did not return. It was a sharp stab like a splinter under a nail: the pain of loss. He would die here under these alien stars, his bones rot in this cold earth.

He had not cried, not for thirty years, not since he was a hungry child too young to know that crying did not fill your belly. But now his throat was thickening, a press of despair behind his eyes forcing warm tears down his cheeks.

There were things worse than dying: life had taught him that. Being here in New South Wales might be one of them.

It seemed at first to be the tears welling, the way the darkness moved in front of him. It took a moment to understand that the stirring was a human, as black as the air itself. His skin swallowed the light and made him not quite real, something only imagined. His eyes were set so deeply into the skull that they were invisible, each in its cave of bone. The rock of his face shaped itself around the big mouth, the imposing nose, the folds of his cheeks. Without surprise, as though he were dreaming, Thornhill saw the scars drawn on the man's chest, each a neat line raised and twisted, living against the skin.

He took a step towards Thornhill so that the parched starlight from the sky fell on his shoulders. He wore his nakedness like a cloak. Upright in his hand, the spear was part of him, an extension of his arm.

Clothed as he was, Thornhill felt skinless as a maggot. The spear was tall and serious. To have evaded death at the end of the rope, only to go like this, his skin punctured and blood spilled beneath these chilly stars! And behind him, hardly hidden by that flap of bark, were those soft parcels of flesh: his wife and children.

Anger, that old familiar friend, came to his side. *Damn your eyes be off*, he shouted. *Go to the devil!* After so long as a felon, hunched under the threat of the lash, he felt himself expanding back into his full size. His voice was rough, full of power, his anger a solid warmth inside him.

He took a threatening step forward. Could make out chips of sharp stone in the end of the spear. It would not go through a man neat as a needle. It would rip its way in. Pulling it out would rip all over again. The thought fanned his rage. *Be off!* Empty though it was, he raised his hand against the man.

The mouth of the black man began to move itself around sounds. As he spoke he gestured with the spear so it came and went in the darkness. They were close enough to touch.

In the fluid rush of speech Thornhill suddenly heard words. *Be off*, the man was shouting. *Be off!* It was his own tone exactly.

This was a kind of madness, as if a dog were to bark in English.

Be off, be off! He was close enough now that he could see the man's eyes catching the light under their heavy brows, and the straight angry line of his mouth. His own words had all dried up, but he stood his ground.

He had died once, in a manner of speaking. He could die again. He had been stripped of everything already: he had only the dirt under his bare feet, his small grip on this unknown place. He had nothing but that, and those helpless sleeping humans in the hut behind him. He was not about to surrender them to any naked black man.

In the silence between them the breeze rattled through the leaves. He glanced back at where his wife and infants lay, and when he looked again the man was gone. The darkness in front of him whispered and shifted, but there was only the forest. It could hide a hundred black men with spears, a thousand, a whole continent full of men with spears and that grim line to their mouths.

He went quickly into the hut, stumbling against the doorway so that clods of daubed mud fell away from the wall. The hut offered no safety, just the idea of it, but he dragged the flap of bark into place. He stretched himself out on the dirt alongside his family, forcing himself to lie still. But every muscle was tensed, anticipating the shock in his neck or his belly, his hand going to the place, the cold moment of finding that unforgiving thing in his flesh.